To the reader of this book ...

Thank you for letting me share
these thoughts of mine with you.

—Dave Malcolm

"This I have come to believe. Racism impacts us all. It diminishes us all. Despite many cosmetic advances during my lifetime, it remains almost as pervasive, intransigent and corrupting today as ever. It is not a simple thing, and we will get nowhere if we persist in trying to deal with it simplistically. It is not simply something that you or I do or don't do, or that the KKK or a Hitler does or doesn't do, or the manufacturers or the bankers or whoever. It is more like a dangerous virus or cancer that has established itself in the body of our social system and is seriously damaging all of our social structures.

"The cycle of racism is self-sustaining, deeply embedded in our past, flourishing in our present, and threatening to our future. Everyone of us who engages in, benefits from, or colludes with any practice of unequal treatment based solely on ethnicity, color, or race--and is apathetic about it--shares in the responsibility for its perpetuation. The challenge racism poses is great; the pain it imposes is greater."

—Chapter Seven

A Whole New Ball Game

A Close-up Look at
Diversity,
Racism, Sexism,
Affirmative Action,
Cultural Pluralism and the
Unfinished Business Remaining in
Twenty-first Century America

Dave Malcolm

Aslan
PUBLISHING
Fairfield, CT

Aslan Publishing
2490 Black Rock Turnpike, #342
Fairfield, CT 06825
Please contact the publisher for a free catalog.
Phone: **203/372-0300**
Fax: **203/374-4766**
www.aslanpublishing.com

Library of Congress Cataloging-in-Publication Data

Malcolm, Dave, 1916-
  A whole new ball game : a close-up look at diversity, racism, sexism,
affirmative action, cultural pluralism and the unfinished business
remaining in twenty-first century America / Dave Malcolm.
     p. cm.
  Includes bibliographical references.
  ISBN 0-944031-98-6
  1. Social perception. 2. Racism. 3. Sexism. 4. Pluralism (social
sciences)—United States. 5. Counselors—Training of—United States. I.
Title.

  HM1071.M35 2005
  305.8'00973—dc22

                              2005045284

Editing and book design by Dianne Schilling
Cover design by Miggs Burroughs
Printing by Baker Johnson, Inc.
Printed in the USA

With gratitude and affection, this book is dedicated. . .

. . .to the memory of the late Ian Duncan Malcolm, my brother and my hero. . . and the other member of an 85-year-long two-brother mutual admiration society that came to an end only with his death in May, 2004.

and

. . .to all my fellow learners, faculty and students in the Community-Based Block program to which I devoted so much of the final nineteen years of my professional life and by which I was so richly rewarded;
. . .to the late George Cox and to Mayo Dansby, both of Tennessee State University, Nashville, who accepted me as a partner in the struggle on behalf of groups underrepresented in higher education despite my obvious white naiveté about peoples of color, and who shepherded me through experiences without which the notion of starting CBB would never have occurred to me;
. . .and to Raymond Howard and Maria Nieto Senour, fellow faculty members who pioneered with me in the early years of CBB and who are like brother and sister and second family to me now.

Acknowledgments

As I look back over the decades of my long life and think about who I was and who I am today, I recognize the contributions made by many others in addition to those to whom this book is dedicated, among them those that I acknowledge below:

—my parents, David J. Malcolm and Mary Lockwood Skinner Malcolm, who faithfully transmitted to me the essence of their white New England Protestant heritage and at the same time encouraged me to question and challenge what I had been taught...

—my two former wives, the late Dr. Virginia Flanagan and Dr. Jean Malcolm, and the late Henry L. Nunn (Virginia's father) whose impacts on my life I have acknowledged in the second chapter...

—my three daughters, Bonnie, River Mary (and her partner, Chris Downing), and Judy; my son Scott; and my stepson Doug Stinson all of whom I love deeply and from all of whom I have learned much, whatever they may or may not have learned from me...

—the late Paul Bruce, the late Jim Carnevale, the late Alice Cochran, Em Cummins, Ralph Miller, and the late John Schmidt—my co-workers in creating a department of counselor education of which we could all feel proud...

—the late Jim Brown (Indiana University), Earl Carnes (University of Southern California), Jack Guthrie (University of Pittsburgh), Pat McGreevy (Arizona State University), and Jim Saum (California State University, Sacramento)—with all of whom early professional association grew into cherished personal friendship...

—the late Carl Rogers, my friend for some twenty-five years with whom it became my good fortune to work particularly closely on his Peace Project during the last three years of his life...

—Claudia Thompson and Rick Gutierrez, my colleagues the first year in the Community-Based Block program who walked with me where others had hesitated to venture...

—the 531 students in the Community-Based Block program during the 19 years that I taught in it from whom I have learned so much and with many of whom I have maintained a continuing personal friendship...

—to Elinor Lobotzke, Maxine Slimmer, and especially to Barbara Hoffman, three remarkable women, each of whom in her way contributed more deeply to my life than I could ever find words to acknowledge...

—and finally I would be remiss if I failed to acknowledge Aslan publishers Harold and Barbara Levine for helping me bring my story to print; CBB graduate Dianne Schilling for editing the manuscript and designing the pages of the book; and graphic artist Miggs Burroughs for creating the cover I imagined and enhancing it tenfold.

—Dave Malcolm

The Blind Men and the Elephant

by John Godfrey Saxe
(1816-1887)

It was six men of Indostan
To learning much inclined,
Who went to see the Elephant
(Though all of them were blind)
That each by observation
Might satisfy his mind.

The First approached the Elephant,
And happening to fall
Against his broad and sturdy side,
At once began to bawl:
"God bless me! but the Elephant
Is very like a wall!"

The Second, feeling of the tusk,
Cried, "Ho! what have we here
So very round and smooth and sharp?
To me 'tis mighty clear
This wonder of an Elephant
Is very like a spear!"

The Third approached the animal
And happening to take
The squirming trunk within his hands
Thus boldly up and spake:
"I see," quoth he, "the Elephant
Is very like a snake!"

The Fourth reached out an eager hand,
And felt about the knee
"What most this wondrous beast is like
Is might plain,'" quoth he;
"'Tis clear enough the Elephant
Is very like a tree!"

The Fifth, who chanced to touch the ear,
Said: "E'en the blindest man
Can tell what this resembles most;
Deny the fact who can
This marvel of an Elephant
Is very like a fan!"

The Sixth no sooner had begun
About the beast to grope,
Then, seizing on the swinging tail
That fell within his scope,,
"I see," quoth he, "the Elephant
Is very like a rope!"

And so these men of Indostan,
Disputed loud and long,
Each in his own opinion
Exceeding stiff and strong,
Though each was partly in the right,
And all were in the wrong!

(based on a fable told in India many years ago)

Contents

Chapter One

A Message from the Writer

During my long lifetime, I have seen enormous cultural change. The larger society and I have journeyed from a world of "Mr. Bones" and "Amos and Andy" and "Stepinfetchit" into a world of Bill Cosby and Martin Luther King and Colin Powell, into a world of La Raza and AIM and Gay Pride and Gender Equity—into a world promising but not yet delivering genuine "equity." Though much progress has been made, much unfinished business still remains. In retrospect it is clear that for the American society into which I was born and of which I will ever be part, the twentieth century can aptly be described as having been one long, continuous, and sometimes painful odyssey into cultural diversity.

This transition from a predominantly white, patently patriarchal, relatively homogeneous and presumably stable social/cultural order into a more pluralistic society is arguably one of the most promising of the legacies that my twentieth century America has bequeathed to our twenty-first century successors. At the same time, it is likely also to prove to be one of the most troublesome and intransigent, one requiring much relearning on the part of Anglo males like myself. As the twenty-first century begins, we white males are finding ourselves in a whole new ball game in which the old ground rules no longer apply. . .and no longer are we the home team. Hence my title for this book. Though much positive change has taken place during my lifetime, the road still ahead will not be easy travelling.

This book is essentially an "open letter" about living with cultural diversity in the twenty-first century, about taking a new look at the unfinished business which the twenty-first century has inherited. It is not written simply to describe my personal experiences, although it is based on them. It is written for white males (like myself) because so much of our whiteness has for so long been invisible to us. . .for women and people of color because so much of this book is about them. . .and for other peoples of difference because so much of what is applicable to gender and color applies to them as well.

Why This Book?

Why do I write this book? Why me? I write this book because, more by chance than by design, life has involved me personally in this cultural transition in a way that has provided me an unusual opportunity to observe and, I think, to learn and understand. Thanks to a series of unplanned and totally unexpected chances, I found both my professional and personal life powerfully impacted by the changes this transition has been bringing—more so, I have reason to believe, than most white males of my generation. My personal odyssey has in many respects been unique in terms of the opportunities it has provided for me to observe diversity in American culture close-up, both through my own eyes and through the eyes of others different from myself. In this book I look back upon my experiences and sort out what I think I have learned from them.

The winds that drove Gulliver off course and plucked Dorothy out of Kansas seem to have governed the directions of my own life as well. Some time after my 54th birthday, the winds of change and chance wafted me out of my secure hitherto largely lily-white world and dropped me down into a small community of diversity in which I was to spend the last two decades of my professional life. Like the larger society within which I lived it, my own life journey became a personal cultural plunge, although admittedly most of my plunge did not take place until quite late in life.

The "community of diversity" into which I was plunged was the Community-Based Block (CBB) program at San Diego State University. CBB was a learning community that, when it started in the early 1970s, was a small island of diversity within what at that time was still virtually an all white university population. It was initially an experimental program—it is still going strong more than thirty years later—and in many ways it was (and still is) both unconventional and controversial within the university setting.

CBB was three faculty members and 20-30 students, two-thirds or more of whom were persons of color, working and learning together as an intact group (hence the term, "block") in a year-long graduate program which for the most part was conducted away from the university campus.

CBB may have been only a small island and an artificial community but still it served as a microcosm of the larger society with most of its attendant social and cultural conflicts. It provided an intense, close-knit and intimate environment in which difficult cultural differences could be acknowledged openly and dealt with honestly by faculty and students alike. It was a place where I saw persons of diverse racial and cultural backgrounds managing not only to live and work together in relative harmony but also to reap much benefit from the experience. The last nineteen years of my professional life were nineteen years of immersion in diversity as a member of this multicultural community, nineteen years of learning to see close-up the diversity in my world, nineteen years of learning to see through new eyes. That is why I presume to write this book.

Deciding What to Include

The story of CBB is a story by itself. Because my years in CBB are such an integral part of who I am today and so much the source of the messages that I have to share, it is difficult for me to believe that a reader can truly understand the ideas and opinions that I have come to hold without first understanding CBB. I still think that way, but after I learned that some persons who had read an early draft of this manuscript and whose reactions otherwise had been highly complimentary had found some of the details about CBB to be a distraction—a view epitomized by the words of one of them who said that whenever he came to "that academic stuff" he sort of "put himself on automatic"—I realized that something needed to be done.

At the same time I was also hearing from other early readers that the parts about CBB seemed to them to be of vital importance. My one-time colleague and long-time friend, the late Dr. Martin Ridge, himself for many years senior editor of a major professional journal, wrote "If for any reason your manuscript itself should not be published, at least the story of CBB deserves to be told. . .as a manuscript it belongs in the SDSU archives."

You see my dilemma.

I had to make a decision. Clearly my primary purpose in writing this "open letter" was to share ideas of mine about cultural differences, ideas that might never have occurred to an Anglo male like me except for my involvement in CBB; it was not to tell the story of that culturally diverse learning community, no matter how influential it may have been as their source. My purpose was to write about diversity in American culture, not about the education of counselors, though both are concerns dear to my heart. My compromise has been to limit mention of CBB in the main text to what I feel is necessary to show what it was about CBB that made it have so great an impact on me and my ideas, and then to add an appendix in which I provide more detail. Those interested in learning more about CBB's origins, processes and outcomes will find more of "that academic stuff" starting on page 151.

How the Book Is Organized

This "open letter" consists of four parts. Part One is about my odyssey as an Anglo male into a strange new world of cultural pluralism. The two chapters tell a little about me and my personal journey and a lot about how I learned to see my world with new eyes. Part Two is about CBB, the island of diversity to which my odyssey took me and the source of so many of the ideas that I express in the two parts that follow. These three chapters tell of the building of a dream and how that dream, in its realization, took on a life of its own and ultimately emerged as the small island of diversity in which I spent much of the last nineteen years of my professional life.

Together Parts One and Two give some sense of where (literally) my ideas are coming from; they deliberately focus for the most part on events and experiences that are in some way related to my exposure (or early lack of exposure) to cultural pluralism.

In the longer third and fourth parts I provide a glimpse into some of the musings about diversity going on inside my head. These are insights and opinions that I have come to hold about diverse matters to which I have given much thought—most of them based on my experience in CBB.

These parts represent an abrupt change from the previous two. This is partly because they are organized by topic instead of by chronology. An even more important difference is that Parts

One and Two were first and foremost a narrative account of external events that were significant in my life and only secondarily an account of what I learned from or thought about them. Parts Three and Four, on the other hand, are first and foremost an account of my internal musings about the significance of those significant events in my life.

The two chapters in Part Three take a look at (1) the confusing profusion of definitions of racism, (2) the self-perpetuating cycles of racism and sexism, (3) white ethnocentrism, and (4) so-called "affirmative action" programs as formal programs necessary to counteract inequities created by informal affirmative action "programs" for white males still existing in American society today.

The four chapters in Part Four examine (1) elusive concepts such as "culture" and "reality," (2) "reality" as viewed by the dominant white male society, and (3) the consequences of cultural differences in how reality is viewed.

In short, Parts One and Two are the story of my travels (*odyssey*); Parts Three and Four are the story of what I found (*diversity*). Together the four parts report the lessons I have learned and tell how, where, when, and why I learned them.[**]

Going Public

This book is my personal story but it is much more than merely a memoir. Despite its informal first-person writing style and its "open letter" format, it has a thoughtful core of important and timely conclusions that I have reached that I present here for consideration and examination.

[**] Part of the chapter about affirmative action was widely reproduced and distributed earlier in the form of an "open letter" which eventually was reprinted in *The Congressional Record* for September 13, 1995.

Permission has been granted to the editors of the *Journal of the Society for Values in Higher Education* (SVHE) to publish a condensed version of the story of my experiences in the Community-Based Block program (Chapters Three, Four, and Five plus Appendix A.)

A limited edition (100 copies) of the first six chapters as they appeared in an early draft of this manuscript was published and distributed under the title *The CBB Story* by a CBB student organization at the time of the graduation of the thirtieth CBB class in May of 2003.

Today as we enter the early years of the twenty-first century, the matters about which I write are all matters about which differences of opinion run deep. I go public with my own musings, not because I believe I offer final answers but in the hope that my experiences, although personal and private, may in some helpful way speak to the experiences of others living in this increasingly complex and interdependent twenty-first century world. I go public on the chance that my ideas just may be ideas that will make a difference. I go public because I think it is important that we take a fresh (and hard) look at the cycles of racism and sexism and what they are doing to our American culture.

During my lifetime, one of the major themes in the story of my Anglo-male world has been its odyssey into diversity. My own parallel life plunge into diversity has taken me into domains that were little known to me beforehand and in which I found rewards far beyond anything I had expected. In 1938, I was a young Harvard graduate dreaming of writing the great American novel. In 2005, I look back and find that instead of writing it, I have been living it.

A Final Note

Most of this book was written after my eightieth birthday. I am keenly aware that the way events may have looked to me in retrospect is not necessarily the way I saw them at the time that they were actually taking place. Whenever possible, I have checked my memories against notes or letters written at the time, or the memories of others. Much I have left out, but whatever I have included I believe to be reasonably free from distortion by my aging memory. Whatever distortions may have crept in despite me, I ask you to accept in the spirit of "I am a part of all that I have met"—that is, that the way I have remembered an event may well be a better indication of the impact it subsequently had upon me than any literal reporting of the actual event itself. In this same spirit, I ask you also to accept the instances in which I have taken license to put direct quotes into my own mouth or the mouths of others.

Throughout the names I have used for all persons mentioned have been their real names unless otherwise indicated, except that in the case of students in all instances the name used is *not* the real name unless otherwise indicated.

Part I

Journey of an Anglo Male

Chapter Two

Roots and Routes

"I am a part of all that I have met."
—Alfred, Lord Tennyson, *Ulysses*

My name is Dave Malcolm and I am an Anglo male. I have been an Anglo male for more than 80 years. The roots I come from and my life during my so-called "formative years" are just about as Anglo and just about as male as you are likely to find.

As far back as I can tell, my ancestors seem to have come from the British Isles. One of my father's great grandparents was a businessman who owned a fleet of fishing vessels sailing out of Wick, Scotland; another was a textile mill manager in Stalybridge, England. My mother's great great great grandfather was a signer of both the Declaration of Independence and the United States Constitution and best known as the author of the Connecticut Compromise. One of her great aunts was the wife of a president of Yale and one of her first cousins was Ted Coy, a legendary football hero at Yale.

I grew up in the 1920s in patriarchal WASP New England in a small town on the Mohawk Trail near the northwest corner of Massachusetts. Some 80 to 90 families lived in the village with roughly the same number in the surrounding area. We had a small Catholic church attended by perhaps a dozen families, mostly from outside of the village, but we didn't know any of them very well except for Bill Hallahan, the town postmaster. Most of the rest of us attended the Protestant church with its tall white steeple visible from afar. There were no people of color in the town, although apparently at one time there must have been at least one because I learned to swim in the Deerfield River at a spot that in my day we all called "Nigger Ed's." Today it is a picnic area along the Mohawk Trail and is known as "Shunpike."

I was raised in a family with two sons and no daughters and a strong proud mother who had given up a successful career as a trained nurse to devote herself totally to taking care of her sons and a husband who'd had polio in early infancy which had left him with a shortened and weakened left leg. I graduated from a 150-year-old, private, all-boys preparatory school and a 300-year-old, all-male ivy league college. It was a family in a community in a region in an era in which gender role expectations were unambiguously defined. It was also a world that was almost exclusively white. Recently I went through my high school and college yearbooks, looking carefully at all the names and all the pictures. I did not find a single non-white face among either the faculty or my classmates at Phillips Exeter. In my Harvard yearbook I found only seven who were identifiable as persons of color—one faculty member (Chinese) and six classmates (three African-Americans, two Japanese, and one Filipino). Try as hard as I can, I do not remember that I ever set eyes on any one of them!

If "Damn Yankee" is one word in parts of the Deep South, when I grew up "Irish Catholic Democratic crook" was one word in our rural rock-ribbed Republican part of Massachusetts. My years at Exeter and Harvard did little to make me question that notion. Until well after I had graduated from college it rarely ever seriously occurred to me that a politician could be a Democrat and still be an honest man. I had grown up in and graduated into an orderly world in which roles were clearly defined and people knew, or at least were expected to "know their place." My own place as a white male Episcopalian in New England, I had been taught, was modestly well up the ladder. Not so high as it would have been if we had been high church Episcopalians instead of low, or had lived on Beacon Hill in Boston or Brattle Street in Cambridge instead of Main Street in small rural Charlemont, or if both of my parents had come from third or fourth generation "old families." But, with a little help from my Exeter and Harvard diplomas, it seemed like a pretty good place from which to start.

At my graduation from Harvard in June of 1938, one of the speakers from the commencement platform welcomed me and my classmates "into the company of educated men." I was soon to find that much of my educating had not yet begun. I was 21 years old. I was sure that I knew exactly what route I was going to follow. I was planning to become a journalist and then I was going to write the great American novel.

At that point in time a writing career for me was a dream that seemed to have some basis in reality. Twenty percent (three) of the fifteen year-long courses that, along with tutorial, made up my entire undergraduate program had been in creative writing. For two of the three, students had to submit samples of their writing to the instructor in advance in order to enroll. One year I was one of only two sophomores among the dozen or so students who were accepted by critic/historian/editor Bernard DeVoto. Another year I was one of only two undergraduates among a similar number of students in the graduate course taught by the poet, Robert Hillyer. Both DeVoto and Hillyer encouraged me to consider writing as a career.

I had no idea then how quickly and how often along the long road ahead that change and chance were to alter my dreams.

My Journey Begins

In 1938 the country was still very much in the depression. After graduation I discovered that the *Boston Herald* was hiring cub reporters at five dollars a week and my plans began to change. Fortunately for me, at that time Massachusetts did not require any special teacher's license or credential to teach in the public schools. Also fortunately, my father was a superintendent of schools and he had lots of friends. I became a public school teacher at $100.00 a month. To my total surprise, it turned out that I liked it very much.

I taught English in a public junior high school for one year. I taught English and Latin and Math in a private boy's prep school for two years. Then I married and moved to Illinois where I taught English in a public high school for one year more. Since I realized that I was soon to be drafted—this was 1941-42—I resigned when school closed and went to work as a newspaper reporter covering the police beat in downtown Chicago while I waited for the draft board to call. My newspaper career lasted for six months, quite long enough to convince me that I much preferred teaching. In November of 1942, I enlisted in the Navy, became an officer, and was assigned to teach navigation at the Midshipmen's School in Chicago where I remained for the duration of the war. Upon discharge early in 1946, I entered Northwestern University under the G. I. Bill and received my Ph.D. in Counseling in August of 1948.

You've Come a Long Way, Baby

By the end of the decade 1938-1948, I had already come a long way on my journey. Events that expanded my horizons had challenged my values and markedly changed my behaviors. Already my world was becoming not what it had seemed to be. Had I been old enough to vote in 1936, I would have voted for Alf Landon over FDR. In 1940, I cast my first presidential ballot—for Republican Wendell Willkie. But in 1944, I voted for Democrat FDR and grieved greatly when he died. And in 1948, I supported and voted for Progressive party candidate Henry Wallace. By 1948, I was an active member of the United World Federalists, the American Civil Liberties Union, and the American Federation of Teachers—all organizations that I would have viewed with suspicion only ten years before.

But it was not my four years of teaching that introduced me to the ideas that expanded my world. Nor was it my newspaper work nor my navy career nor my doctoral program. Each of these no doubt made its contribution, but I doubt if anything I was exposed to or called upon to do in any of them would necessarily have changed me greatly from the person I had been in 1938. The catalyst for change was my marriage, or, more accurately, the remarkable woman to whom I was married and, to almost as great an extent, her remarkable father, a prominent industrialist, founder and CEO of the Nunn-Bush shoe company who was pro-union, an ardent Democrat, and widely known for his innovative and unorthodox "Share Production" views on labor-management relations.

At the time we were married, Virginia Nunn was already a Radcliffe Phi Beta Kappa with her master's degree in Philosophy and about to enter a Ph.D. program at the University of Chicago. She had a thirst for learning and a hunger for new ideas that I have rarely seen matched. After a quarter or two, she found the specialization of a doctoral program in philosophy to be too confining for her wide ranging interests and left to become one of the first two women to be hired as a newspaper reporter in Chicago to replace the men who were being called into military service. (It was through her influence that I got my chance to be a reporter!)

Two years later Virginia returned to the University of Chicago to complete an undergraduate pre-med program and then entered medical school at the University of Illinois. She continued to push boundaries in her search for and discovery of new things to study as long as she lived. Virginia died on the last day of December 1996 in a hospital in Tijuana, Mexico, to which she had gone, still continuing her lifelong search for and study of the new and the lesser known, this time for non-traditional treatments in her own battle with cancer.

During the course of our fifteen years of life together, thanks to her wide-ranging interests and her restless energy, I was exposed to a variety of *au courant* social, political, and economic views, many of which I might never have heard of on my own. From the beginning, our lifestyle was a compromise between my small town needs for conforming to conventional mores and her endless struggle for personal and professional survival against the shackles of a male-dominated world. She was politically liberal and pro-union. She introduced me to the songs of Woody Guthrie and Pete Seeger and Paul Robeson and Josh White. She was far ahead of her time—she used her maiden name for the first four years of our marriage (almost scandalous behavior at that time), changing only when our first child was born. When the first child arrived, we studied the pioneering work of Arnold Gesell at the Yale Child Study Center. Later she was one of the first to become familiar with the writings of Dr. Benjamin Spock.

Our relationship was very unusual in those days—this was more than fifty years ago—and, try as hard as I can, I cannot recall knowing even one other couple with a relationship at all similar to ours. Those who knew us considered us not only to be unusual but also a very remarkable couple. We both were active and successful professionals. I assumed a substantial part of the parenting while she combined both home and career. (At the time, in my naiveté, I took pride in the praise I was getting for doing perhaps 20 to 25 percent of the parenting, not noticing until much later that people were not praising her and she was doing 75 percent or more of it!)

Long before the lonely struggles of women like Virginia had blossomed into the feminist movement, I was slowly becoming sensitized to my own insensitivity. The more I came face to face with the obvious inequities, the more my loyalty to conventional views began to fade. Thanks to my wife and my father-in-law, I had come a long way in ten years in terms of my political and social attitudes and activism. But for all my activism and the increasing liberalization of my views, my world remained virtually lily-white. There was one African-American enrolled in the doctoral program at Northwestern at the same time that I was; he was the first person of color that I can remember with whom I had even casual contact over any extended period of time. I was already in my thirties by then!

Moving Right Along

In 1948 I left Northwestern, brand new Ph.D. in hand, to take a position at what is now the University of Wisconsin in Milwaukee (UWM). For five years I taught psychology and counseling and supervised prospective secondary school teachers in their practice teaching. In 1953, the family moved to California where I assumed similar duties at San Diego State College (now "University"). My idea at the time was to work in California for a few years and then to move along. Wrong, very wrong. In 1992, thirty-nine years later, I was still there, still teaching at SDSU.

After the move to California, life brought many changes. In 1956, after fifteen years, my marriage ended in divorce. Despite our demanding professional careers and our commitment to social and political activism, Virginia and I had always tried to make sure that the concerns of our four children came first. Now our closely-knit, child-centered family was shattered and scattered. The change was hard on the children, hard on Virginia, and hard on me. At about this time, I was placed in charge of developing the counselor education program at SDSU and I responded by becoming more deeply immersed in my professional work than I had ever let myself become before.

Two years later I remarried. My second wife, like my first, was a professional person in her own right. Jean Stinson also completed a doctoral program (Ph.D., not M.D.) during the years that we were married. She provided me with support at home without which it would not have been possible for me to have become as involved in professional activities and to accomplish all the things that I did. My writing skills now stood me in good stead. Within a matter of a very few years, I was writing grant proposals that competed successfully for funding in competition with larger and more prestigious universities.

I was assuming a leadership role in my profession and serving in a variety of elective and appointive positions at state and national levels, and I was enjoying a considerable level of respect and status among my peers. For six consecutive years I was elected to the executive council of the Association for Counselor Education and Supervision (ACES), the national organization for counselor educators, and for those same years served as an ACES delegate to the senate of our umbrella organization, the American Personnel and Guidance Association, now the American Counseling Association.

My life was also enriched by Jean's love for travel. We went together to Egypt and the Holy Land, to East Africa, to Europe, to Russia and Siberia, to Alaska, to Jamaica and the Virgin Islands, to Mexico and Central and South America, to New Zealand and Australia—all places I greatly enjoyed once I got there yet probably never would have gotten to on my own.

In many respects, the years during my second marriage were very rewarding ones for me. I had opportunities to do many things and meet many people and I am grateful for them all. I traveled frequently to Washington, D. C., and made numerous presentations before committees of the California legislature in Sacramento. I traveled extensively around the country attending meetings and serving as a consultant. In one role or another, I visited the campuses of most of the major universities in this country. I was appreciated and I was well received. I made a number of valued friends among my professional associates. All the same, I can look back now and see that my successes during those years, rewarding as they were, came only at a price. I rarely stayed long enough in any one place to become truly intimately involved with the persons with whom I worked. With a few important exceptions, my relationships, though valued, were necessarily superficial.

As my professional involvement increased, I noticed that my social and political activism diminished. Even in the vacation travel with Jean that I now value so much, I was more passive spectator than participant. The rewards during those years were many and I do not mean to denigrate them, but at the same time something important seemed to be lacking. (And my friends and associates and students were still almost all white.)

At a Turning Point

The turning point came in the summer of 1970. That summer I, an Anglo male university professor, now almost 54 years old, was about to take off on sabbatical leave. I had been profoundly influenced by the events of the 1960s, especially by the idealism of the youth of the '60s, among them my oldest children, who were involved in the counter culture movement and who, it seemed to me, in so many ways were actually trying to put into practice what I and my generation had only preached. (And the adult society of my generation tried to destroy them because they did!) I had been similarly influenced by my graduate students in counselor education who, it so frequently turned out, knew and could do things that I and other faculty knew little or nothing about.

My children and my students belonged to a world strange and new to me. They were into Carlos Castaneda, the I Ching, Zen, Sufi, American Indian lore, Tai Chi, psychedelics, Esalen, Eastern religions, Marcuse, Anais Nin, Ram Dass, Lorca, Theodore Roszak, Ken Kesey, Alvin Toffler, Ivan Illich, Paulo Freire, the Beatles and the Beats—realms unnervingly unfamiliar to me and to my peers. I found myself sharing their dreams. As I left on my sabbatical, I was increasingly uncomfortable with the idea of returning to the conventional faculty role that defined my relationship with students strictly as one in which they should come to learn from me, when I now strongly suspected that often I had as much or more to learn from some of them.

Officially, my sabbatical plan was to study the alternative social structures developing in the youth culture of the late 1960s—the communes, the free schools, the underground press, the experimental colleges. Privately, my hope was that this study would lead me to a career change, help me to find a setting more congenial than the traditional professorial role had become.

I found congenial situations enough but I also quickly found that there was no place for someone like me, that at my age and with my background I had little or nothing to contribute. But even while I was discovering this hard truth, events elsewhere were taking place that would sweep me up and carry me in certain new and unexpected directions that were to become my major interest for the remainder of my professional life.

In Washington, D. C., though Nixon was now president, civil rights continued to be a top priority. The branch of the U.S. Office of Education (USOE) that had been funding counselor education programs was now introducing a new funding model, one that (among other things) was designed both to strengthen programs at institutions that previously had been unable to compete successfully for funds, and to bring "more members of underrepresented groups" (code words for "people of color") into graduate level training programs.[1] Since in some instances this meant making grants to institutions with little or no prior experience in managing federally funded contracts, it was decided that the services of an external consultant should be provided. I was on sabbatical leave so I was available. I was experienced and I was well regarded in the Office of Education. During the decade of the 1960s, I had received USOE grants and contracts totaling approximately $3,000,000—this would be perhaps ten times that much in twenty-first century dollars.[2]

My grants had made me highly visible. Not only was I one of a very small number of persons in my profession who had been the recipient of anything close to this amount, I was the only one teaching at a university that did not offer the doctoral degree in my field. I had been employed by the USOE as a consultant before. In fact, by this time I had become part of a small but influen-

---

[1] For more detail about this model, see my article, "The Center/Satellite Model: Grand Strategy for Change," *Personnel and Guidance Journal*, 52:303-308 (January 1974).

[2] Even at the end of that decade (1969) a movie ticket typically cost $1.00 or less, a new Ford car about $2,200, and a three-bedroom home around $19,000. Postage for mailing a first class letter had just been increased from five cents to six and at most colleges, including SDSU, the top annual salary for a full professor was $15,000 or below.

tial "good-old-boys" network—all of us white males, of course.
Result: midway through my sabbatical year, I became an external
consultant. Apparently, no one, including me, had given much
thought to the fact that I had no expertise nor prior experience in
working with people of color. Truly, I was in for a cultural plunge!
Truly, my relearning was far from done!

An American Life

Until I wrote the preceding chronology, I had never fully
realized the extent to which the forces and events that were changing American life in general were the forces and events that had
been shaping mine. I had attended an all-male private boarding
school and an all-male ivy league college at a time when this was
what virtually any boy did who could possibly do so. My boyhood was spent in a rural community (village population about
350); my adult life has been spent primarily in metropolitan Boston, Chicago, Milwaukee, and San Diego. Depression salaries in
the 1930s turned me away from the profession of journalism and
into teaching. The start of World War II gave me a chance to taste
the life of a journalist after all; the GI Bill paid for my doctorate.
The pre-war New Deal helped shape my values and my politics;
the post-war new freedoms for women enriched my married life.
The various movements of the Sixties, and the involvement of my
students and of my own children in them, brought the most dramatic changes of all. The listing could go on and on. Clearly I am
a product of my place and my time. As I wrote earlier in this
book, my life was shaped by the forces and events out of which
the great American novel might have been made.

Curiously, the forces and events that were ultimately to have
the greatest impact of all on my life, the civil rights movement
and the increasing diversification of the population in America,
had left me virtually untouched for the first fifty-four years of my
life. Now, in my mid-fifties, this was about to change. I like to
refer to the next few years as my "baptism by immersion." In
Chapter Three I will explain what I mean.

Chapter Three

Seeing with New Eyes

*"The real voyage of discovery consists not in seeking new landscapes
but in having new eyes."*
—Marcel Proust

Naive as I was about working with people of color, early in
1971 I took on the USOE job as external consultant to what came
to be known as its "Center/Satellite Program," extended my leave
for an additional year and suddenly found myself embarking on
the journey that would make the next twenty years of my personal and professional life so stimulating and so rewarding. In the
course of my duties I worked with Chicanos in the southwest,
Native American Indians in the northwest, and African-Americans
in a number of large eastern and north central urban centers.
However, most of my time was spent with the Southeast Regional
Center at Tennessee State University (TSU) in Nashville and its
satellites in Alabama, Florida, Georgia, Mississippi and Tennessee
which was unique in that each satellite involved two universities—one traditionally black and one traditionally white. (For example, in Mississippi the universities involved were white "Ole
Miss" at Oxford and black Jackson State.) The year and a half that
followed was packed with new experiences. Despite my numerous blunders and naïveté about people of color (I had never even
heard of Marvin Gaye!), my work as a consultant turned out to be
both satisfying and successful.

My sabbatical leave had taken me to the University of Pittsburgh where friendly colleagues had provided me with an office

and a temporary part-time appointment. My calendar shows that during most of the next year and a half, I was away from Pittsburgh as much time as I was at home. I had often served as a consultant before, but it had never been like this. Always before, I had prepared thoroughly, had a good plan, and knew how I was going to carry it out. I put on a good show. Usually I received gratifying compliments and often I was invited back. Sometimes I had the disquieting suspicion that not much had happened as a result, but I never really knew. This time was different. I met with the same people over and over again. I traveled with them from site to site. Often I stayed in their homes and went to their parties. More often than not, I had no time to prepare or plan—I simply met with people, got involved, and little by little began to make suggestions or share ideas, often ideas that I had picked up only a few days before while visiting at some other university. Now I knew when and if my contributions had made any difference. Much of the time they had. But as I look back now, it is not my consulting successes that make those days so memorable. Instead, the events that stand out most vividly in my memory are a number of powerful personal experiences from which I learned much about myself and during which I began to see myself and my white world from a side from which I had never looked at it before. It was as if I were seeing my world with new eyes. Several examples are reported in the pages that follow.

En Route to Ole Miss

One of these memorable learning experiences came on one of my first trips into the south. I was en route to a meeting at the University of Mississippi at Oxford. I flew from Pittsburgh to Memphis where I met Professor Mayo Dansby, chair of the department of psychology at TSU and co-director of the Nashville center. We had reserved a rental car for the hour and a half drive to Oxford. It was one of the longest 90-minute drives of my life. We had scarcely crossed the state line into Mississippi when a pickup truck passed us, slowed down and pulled over, then passed us again. The second time it passed I noticed the gun in the gun rack in the cab rear window. At that moment I became acutely aware of the fact that I was a white man driving with an African-American woman in the state of Mississippi—not too far away from the area where the bodies of the three murdered young freedom riders had been found only a few years before. Not surprisingly, Dr. Dansby was even more tense than I. For the rest of the drive, I was torn between trying to drive with meticulous care in order to avoid accidents or violations and the mad desire to speed up to get more quickly to the safety of our destination.

We made the trip both ways without incident. The return trip was as tense as the trip down. I don't think I had ever noticed more pickups on the highway. I don't think I just imagined that the looks we received were more than merely disapproving. It made no difference that Dr. Dansby was the co-director of an important educational center, a respected professor and administrator at an important university, the daughter of a university president, and one of the first African-American women to earn her Ph.D. in psychology. Her background and her credentials were no protection for either her or me. Both of us literally breathed easier when we finally re-crossed the state line into Tennessee. On this short trip I had gotten my first small gut-level sense of what life would have been like for me if I had been born African-American in Mississippi. I have no way of knowing how much reality there was for my fears that day—even a little reality would have been justification enough. I do know the fear I felt was real.

Way Down in New Orleans

On another occasion, I attended a meeting in Biloxi, Mississippi, that had been scheduled to last for two full days but which actually ended mid-morning on the second day. I was traveling with the late Dr. George Cox, later vice president (and for one year, acting president) at TSU, but at that time co-director of the Nashville Center. Since we were not scheduled to fly out of New Orleans until late that evening, George and I and four others decided to cancel our reservations on the late afternoon commuter flight and drive to New Orleans in a rental car instead. I was the only white in the group.

Somewhere en route, my companions decided they wanted some genuine New Orleans soul food. Once we were in downtown New Orleans, one of them spoke to a taxi driver alongside of us as we were stopped for a red light. He told him what we were looking for and asked for suggestions. The light changed at that moment and traffic started moving, but the taxi driver motioned to us to follow him, which we did. Now I had been in New Orleans a number of times before, but I was not prepared for the section into which he took us. Even my African-American companions were beginning to have doubts. But before we could turn back, the taxi driver stopped in front of a two-story building with a restaurant downstairs and a noisy bar on the floor above. It was still early, so we went first to the bar upstairs. As we went inside, I was only too aware that I had not seen a white face for what seemed like ten or fifteen minutes.

The tables and booths were crowded so our group took stools at the bar. Almost immediately I became aware of an urgent need to urinate. I held out as long as I thought I safely could, hoping that George or one of the other men in our group would have the same urge. Apparently no one did. I thought of asking someone to accompany me, but my pride held me back. Besides, all five were noisily engaged in a discussion about soul food with the bartender. Everyone was talking at once and speaking so rapidly that I couldn't fully understand them, and I was reluctant to interrupt. I decided I had to prove something and go by myself. After all, if I didn't come back soon, George would surely notice. I might be beaten up but I probably wouldn't be dead. I steeled myself for the ordeal and, looking neither right nor left, I went. The whole trip was uneventful. Later I sheepishly confessed to what I had gone through. Amidst the good-natured kidding that ensued there was a serious note. Now, they told me, I knew a little about what it was like to be African-American in a world that so often was all white.

Tour of Harlem

On another occasion, George Cox and I attended a two-day conference at Queens College, a satellite of the Center at the University of Pittsburgh. It was school vacation time and George had brought along his two adolescent daughters who had never been to New York City before. Since George was heavily scheduled the first day and I had an open afternoon, I agreed to take our rental car and show his two youngsters around the famous city. Many years before, back in my undergraduate days, I had become quite familiar with the city and now it quickly came back to me as I drove them along Broadway and Fifth Avenue, through Times Square, past the Empire State Building, over the Brooklyn Bridge and back, and into Central Park. Things were going so smoothly that when they said that what they wanted to see most was Harlem, I was pretty certain that I could find it even though I had never been there. So off we went. I found it without difficulty and as I drove around the girls spotted several landmarks they recognized. At one point, as I was about to make a right turn, I noticed just in time that the street was blocked off by half a dozen or more police cars. That made me a little nervous but it was just one more added attraction for the girls. Harlem was the high point of their tour.

We returned triumphantly to pick up George at the end of his afternoon meeting and adjourned with half a dozen or more others to somebody's hotel room to relax and have a beer. Once again, I found myself the only white person in the room. The girls, of course, took center stage. They could scarcely wait to tell about having been to Harlem. The reaction they got was not what they—or I—had expected. For the first time, I saw the scene through African-American eyes—a white man in a new model car with two attractive young light-skinned nubile African-American girls. My friends were partly kidding me, partly truly thankful that we hadn't gotten into serious trouble. There was some disagreement about which had been my biggest danger—the cops arresting me as a pimp, or African-American youths beating me up for the same reason.

An Evening in Austin

The experiences I have described above were all positive experiences for me in the sense that I learned important lessons about myself and about my world even though the situations in which my learning took place were themselves, if not negative, at least somewhat unpleasant ones. Equally powerful learnings frequently came from peak moments in pleasant situations. An evening I spent in Austin, Texas, is a case in point.

At nine or ten o'clock, after a long and exhausting day of meetings at the University of Texas (sponsored by the Southwestern Center at The University of New Mexico), a group of ten or twelve of us gathered together in one of the rooms at our hotel. The group was all male and consisted mainly of Chicano faculty members and graduate students from various southwestern universities, except that Dusty Wilson from the USOE in Washington and I had been invited to come along. Although drinks were available, there was little or no drinking and there was no postmortem discussion of the events of the day. Instead, two of the men got out guitars and one of the magic moments of my life followed.

It is impossible for me to recapture that magic in words and I will not try to do so. The singing lasted for an hour or two, perhaps more. Sometimes others in the room joined in the singing, sometimes only the guitar players sang. Some of the songs were in English, some were in Spanish, and a few were a mixture. Some songs were slow and some were lively, some were sad and some were happy. Some were humorous. Many were love songs. Few if any of them were familiar to me. If my memory is correct, one song that I heard for the first time that night was "La Bomba" although this was many years before Los Lobos was to make the song so famous. I seem to recall that it was repeated over and over until even I, with my limited Spanish, recognized "Yo no soy marinaro" and could join in on parts of the chorus. But knowing the songs or their words was not important. All the songs were songs of feeling. All were sung with emotion. The entire evening I felt bathed in emotion—my own and the singers' and everyone else's present.

When the evening ended, Dusty Wilson and I walked together slowly and silently toward our rooms. At the end of the corridor where we turned in opposite directions, we mumbled "Good night's" and continued on our ways. I had gone but a few steps when Dusty called to me. I turned and he said softly, "Dave, who is really disadvantaged?" I know of no better way to say it. What I had actually felt and learned doesn't lend itself to being captured easily in words. Dusty's comment at least gives some hint of how that magical evening felt to us. Dusty and I had been like waifs standing outside with our noses pressed against the windowpane looking at the warmth and wealth inside. I knew it, and Dusty knew it too.

I do not remember that I ever saw Dusty again after that conference and I had barely known him before it, but ever since that night, any time I hear someone speak derogatorily of "faceless Washington bureaucrats," I think of that special evening Dusty and I shared in Austin. . .and I wish the speaker could have known Dusty Wilson.

A Panel at D-QU

Deganawidah-Quetzalcoatl University (D-QU) was (and still is, I presume) a cooperative Native American Indian-Chicano university located in Davis, California. Although D-QU was not itself a part of our center/satellite program, it was a convenient and logical location for a workshop sponsored jointly by the northwestern (Indian) and southwestern (Chicano) centers. One panel at that workshop still remains a vivid memory.

The panel topic was "The Role of the Native American Indian Woman today." The panel members were six young Native American Indian women, all of whom, if my memory doesn't fail me, were in their late twenties or early thirties. In the discussion, they were divided three and three. Three of them argued eloquently and cogently that it was imperative that Native American Indian women continue in their traditional tribal roles because the preservation and transmittal of traditional tribal culture and values depend on it; the other three argued equally eloquently and equally cogently that the time had come for Indian women to be freed from the shackles of tribal traditions and to take their places as equals in the world alongside their brothers. As I listened, I realized that, at least for me, both sides were right, both arguments were irrefutable. These women were living simultaneously in two realities, equally "real" yet irreconcilable.

This was not the first time in my life—nor would it be the last—that I discovered two mutually contradictory ideas both alive and well and thriving side by side within my head. This instance was particularly poignant because I left that meeting with such enormous respect for the six women, each of whom had so obviously spoken from her heart, each of whom had so clearly understood and fully shared the values of the others, each of whom had arrived at the position she espoused only at the cost of deep and painful personal search. I left with a sadness that comes echoing back again as I write these lines these many years later. There was and is no answer. Their two worlds still remain in head-on collision.

W. E. B. DuBois expressed his own Black sense of this "twoness" nearly a century earlier when, speaking of himself in the third person, he wrote "One ever feels his twoness—an American, a Negro; two souls, two thoughts, two unreconciled strivings; two warring ideals in one dark body, whose dogged strength alone keeps it from being torn asunder." [3]

At D-QU six fine young persons had bared their personal anguish and in so doing they had given me a glimpse into what life is like inside the dual reality in which persons of color live, a glimpse that I might otherwise never have seen so clearly. Many times when it has been important for me to do so, the memory of this panel has helped me to keep in mind how little I can really ever know about what it is like to grow up in this country in a non-white skin.

A Weekend in Nashville

If, as I like to claim, my introduction into the world of people of color was "baptism by total immersion," it was George Cox who administered the sacrament. George and I worked together well from the start. In a sense, we faced similar situations. George, previously a successful public school administrator in Memphis, had been newly hired at TSU specifically for the co-director position and in many ways he found the worlds of higher education and federal finance to be almost as new and alien to him as the world of color was to me. I helped him to negotiate his way in academe and Washington; he tolerated with friendly amusement my numerous cultural missteps and blunders, and his friends accepted me more readily because of him. Our symbiotic professional relationship rapidly evolved into a close personal friendship. We began to share the same hotel room, though our separate travel budgets would have paid for individual rooms. We shared each other's personal hopes and struggles as openly as we did our professional ones. Every time I flew into Nashville, George

---

[3] "The Souls of Black Folk" (1903). Reprinted in *Three Negro Classics*, Avon Books, New York, 1965, p. 215.

made it a point to be the person to meet me at the airport, each time taking great delight in greeting me by handing me a brown paper bag containing a cold bottle of Michelob. By the time my leave of absence was nearing its end, I considered George to be one of the closest of my adult male friends. Clearly the feelings were mutual.

Shortly before my scheduled return to San Diego, I spent a weekend with George in his home in Nashville where he lived alone while his daughters were with his divorced wife. On Friday we had finished a workshop in Nashville and the following Monday we were scheduled to fly together to repeat the same workshop at the satellite in Atlanta. George also invited two of our fellow workshop presenters, two young African-Americans from the San Francisco Bay area, to stay with us. The two were barely half my age—I was 56 and they were in their very early thirties, if that. (George was almost exactly halfway between.) Despite the disparity in our ages, the weekend was a great success. We watched sports on TV together, we went on a boisterous shopping trip to buy supplies for barbecues on Saturday and Sunday nights. We were playful and often loud. We told stories and we argued and we disagreed, all with great good humor. I enjoyed myself thoroughly and I do not recall a tense moment during the entire two days.

And yet. . .and yet there were moments when I was an outsider though I never felt deliberately excluded. Even though George and the other two did not know each other very well, I could sense some special bond between them that George and I, as close as we were, would never share. A very obvious manifestation of it was the practice among African-American males, popular at that particular time, of greeting each other as "Nigger"—as in "Hey, nigga, any more coffee in that pot?" But it was more than that, something subtler and broader, something that would have been there even if that particular usage of the n-word had not been in vogue at the time. I did not have the feeling that this in any way diminished the special closeness that George and I shared. My relationship with George was something that probably neither of them would ever attain. The difference was that my friendship with George was built slowly out of our personal interactions over time; theirs was almost instant, almost as if by birthright. This was an important thing for me as a white man to know.

Sunday evening, after we were well fed and relaxing around the dinner table, I decided to bring the subject up. I said, probably in pretty much these very words, "You know, this has been a great weekend and all that, but in one way you bastards have been doing me no favor the way you've been calling each other 'nigger this' and 'nigger that' because now I may slip and use it and sometimes it may be OK but sometimes not." Although I had mostly addressed my comment to George, one of the younger men answered. Switching into the black speech pattern that African-Americans usually reserve for speaking to each other, he told me, "Tha's right, white boy, and wha's more, you ain't neva gonna know which time is which." The wisdom of that statement, I have many times observed, is one of the hardest truths for most whites who work with people of color to accept.

A Visit to Rocky Boy

The last of the "memorable experiences" that I want to describe was a week-long visit to an Indian reservation in north central Montana between Great Falls and Havre. I include it here even though it did not take place until the first week in May in the spring after my return to San Diego State University.

George Cox and I and some 25 to 30 persons from the Nashville Center's satellites, about two-thirds of them African-Americans, spent a week on Rocky Boy's Reservation as part of a cultural exchange arranged by George and our friend Rick LaPointe. Rick, whose Indian name was Two Horse, by this time had become George's counterpart at the Northwestern (Native American Indian) Center at the University of South Dakota. (Because of my friendship with George and Rick, I had agreed to continue to serve as a consultant to both centers even after my return to SDSU.) Rick told us that Rocky Boy's Reservation was the smallest and probably the poorest reservation in Montana. It had been named for a Chief Rocky Boy whose Indian name, we were told, would have been more accurately translated as "Stone Child." Rick and George had originally intended our visit to take place at Wounded Knee in South Dakota but conflict between government officials and Native Americans there had turned violent and it would not have been safe. Rocky Boy was chosen as replacement because Rick knew it well, having recently worked there for a year as an intern during his graduate study.

The visit did not start out well. We were greeted politely but coolly by the tribal elders. It was clear that we were there only as a special favor to Rick of whom they were obviously very fond. We were told, for example, that a pow-wow scheduled for the middle of the week was an Indian ceremony to which outsiders were not invited. Our hosts remembered their history all too well. Following the Civil War, freed slaves had become the "buffalo soldiers" who had played a major role in crushing the Indians as white settlers moved west. But the coolness did not last long. It was the Indian children who broke the ice. They were fascinated by the massive "Afro" hair-do's sported by some of the African-American males in our group. I can still picture some six-foot male seated on a step or rock, bending way over so some delighted three- or four-year-old could use his "pick" to comb his hair. Each of the African-American males became a pied piper, followed wherever he went by his own little group of admiring children. Result: not only were we warmly welcomed to the mid-week pow-wow after all, but an additional pow-wow was held in our honor on the night before we left. Clearly by week's end we were outsiders no longer.

The highlight for me was a sweat lodge experience on our final day. We were invited to take part in a sweat in the personal sweat lodge of one of the elders, Sam Windyboy, Sr. We were told that if we were Indian, we would be expected to fast for twenty-four hours in advance but in our case we could take part as long as we did not come just to observe, but ready to participate in it as a religious experience. About fifteen of us accepted the invitation. We were advised to wear a minimum of loose-fitting clothing and given wet towels to hold to our faces in the event the steam became too hot. We watched the hot rocks being brought from the fire pit outside and placed into the pit dug in the ground in the center of the sweat lodge. George and Rick and I and the others crawled into the tiny, crowded interior, joining Mr. Windyboy, Sam, Jr., and a third Indian male whom I had not seen before. Mr. Windyboy explained to us that there would be prayers and chanting and speeches and drumming and that we were encouraged to join in. He showed us the buffalo horn which he would dip into a pail beside him to toss water onto the heated rocks. He advised us that if the steam got too hot to put our faces near the ground—almost an impossibility the way we were crowded together. He told us that there would be two or three breaks for air. Then someone outside dropped the tarpaulin over the entrance (in the old days the tarpaulins would have been buffalo hides) and we were plunged into absolute darkness.

The ceremony started with drumming and chanting punctuated by bursts of steam each time another hornful of water was tossed onto the rocks. With each additional burst, the steam became hotter and hotter. As the heat rose, even with my wet towel at my face, I had to bend as near to the ground as possible in order barely to survive. Finally Mr. Windyboy began his prayers. He spoke of "broken promises" and "the buffalo are gone" as if it had been only yesterday, but his prayers were not prayers of rancor but of deep sorrow—prayers that the Great Spirit would help the white man to see the error of his ways and stop his destruction of Mother Earth. Then the tarpaulin was removed from the entrance and cool water and blueberries preserved the summer before were passed around. When we resumed after the break, we learned that the stranger I had noticed was an apprentice medicine man and that this was his last sweat before his vision-quest ordeal, which would involve being tied for four days in the mountains. The prayers this time were for strength for the apprentice. The details seemed rather vague, perhaps deliberately so, since the practice was considered to be illegal by white authorities.

After another break and more water and blueberries, the third segment began with Rick replying to Mr. Windyboy who, he said, had been his second "father" during his year at Rocky Boy. He thanked his "father" for this sweat, saying he particularly had needed it at this time to give him strength because he had recently lost his grandfather. He had also lost his cousin who had been more like a brother, only a few days different from him in age and raised in the same household, who had died the previous Friday, killed at Wounded Knee.[4] That triggered something so deep in me that I completely fell apart. I have never experienced

---

[4] Rick's "brother" was killed at Wounded Knee on Friday, April 27, 1973.

anything like it. I felt as if I were a shapeless pool spreading out on the ground. I don't know how to describe it. I don't think it was collective guilt (though it may have been). It seemed more a sense of "oneness," a sense that I was Rick and his cousin, and every Indian and every white man who had ever lived, and the buffalo, and all other living creatures, and I was crying and crying and lying there on the ground. Then came more cool water and more berries and I think that was the end of the sweat. If there was a fourth segment, I do not remember it.

Afterwards I felt a great feeling of serenity and inner peace. I went off by myself, climbed perhaps 100 feet up a hillside and sat silently and watched the scene below. I watched others walking around alone or in pairs, except for two who had climbed the hillside and were sitting alone like I was. In time I noticed people beginning to drift back together and I felt a strong need to join them so I came down from the hill. For a long time after I returned to the group, I stayed at the edge. I knew that I wasn't ready to talk yet.

Hours later some of the group were talking about their experiences but it would still be a long time before I felt ready to try to talk about mine. Even now, years later, I still do not understand it at all. I did talk to the persons who had been on either side of me to see if they had noticed anything curious about my reactions. In the total darkness they had not noticed a thing. The next day sitting in the Great Falls airport with George and Rick and Sam Windyboy, Jr., I mentioned that during one of the earlier segments I had experienced the feeling that I was flying, floating rapidly and effortlessly, and I could look down and see hills and roads and bushes and occasional patches of late April snow as they passed below, and that, interestingly enough, in the total darkness I could see the images equally well whether my eyes were closed or open. Rick and Sam Jr. looked at each other and one of them said aside to the other, "The spirits took him." I have never forgotten that comment, nor the quiet, almost reverent tone in which it was spoken.

Rick's comment came flooding back to me several years later. While rereading *Black Elk Speaks,* I came to a passage that left me stunned (and awe stricken!) to find my own experience vividly and accurately described by Black Elk in his description of his own "flying" during his sacred vision quest.

"I must have fallen down, but I felt as though I had fallen off a swing when it was going forward, and I was floating head first through the air . . . My body did not move at all, but I looked ahead and floated fast toward where I looked. There was a ridge right in front of me, and I thought I was going to run into it, but I went right over it. On the other side of the ridge I could see a beautiful land where many people were camping. . ." [5]

As I look back on that year and a half, I still find it hard to understand how one as naive and as inexperienced in working with people of color as I was managed to survive at all, much less to be so generously accepted and so generally successful. No doubt my acceptance and survival were due in large part to the attitude with which I came to the job. At that particular moment in my life I had been ready to abandon the professorial role with which I had become increasingly so uncomfortable. I had come realizing that I had much to learn from the people with whom I was to work while at the same time not at all certain how relevant the things I knew would be to them, but hoping I could contribute something worthwhile. I had not appreciated the wisdom of this approach in advance and it is not something that I can take any credit for having planned. It was just my great good fortune to have the opportunity come at exactly the time in my life when it did. And the cumulative impact of these experiences and others like them would influence the rest of my professional life. What's more, though I doubt if I fully realized it at the time, it was certainly the beginning of my seeing my world with new eyes.

Clearly I did learn a great deal from those with whom I worked; equally clearly, I did make a contribution which was valued by them since they continued to retain my services as a part-time consultant for several semesters after my leave had ended. (The week at Rocky Boy that I described and a subsequent visit both took place later, for example.) It had been a symbiotic relationship. They had known things I wouldn't have known and I had known things they wouldn't have known and together we

---

[5] *Black Elk Speaks,* Simon & Schuster, New York, Pocket Book Edition, 1972, p. 205.

became a productive partnership. And, with a little help from my friends—like George Cox and Mayo Dansby—I had had a wonderful time in the process.

My leave ended at the end of the summer of 1972 and it was with mixed feelings that I prepared to return to San Diego State. I had left reluctant ever again to resume the traditional hierarchical faculty-student role relationship. But now that I realized how satisfying and productive a symbiotic/partnership relationship could be, a new dream was beginning to emerge—a dream of teaching in a program in which this same partnership would exist between faculty and students. The details were far from clear in my mind but at least I knew the role that I wanted to play and that I wanted it to involve people of color. I returned to San Diego dreaming of trying to create this role for myself within the university yet at the same time filled with uneasiness about how to do it and about whether the university could and would accept it.

Would it all be only a dream?

Part II

An Island of Diversity

Chapter Four

The Dream and the Reality

"How can I go forward when I don't know
which way I'm facing?
How can I go forward when I don't know
which way to turn?
How can I go forward in something I'm not sure of..."
—John Lennon (from "How" on his album *Imagine*)

When I returned to San Diego State University in the fall of 1972, I was not yet 56 years old. I had come home with a dream. The travels of my sabbatical years may have been over but my odyssey into diversity was far from finished. The final destination of my odyssey—the diverse learning community of my dream—did not yet exist. This was the year that would determine whether it ever would. My dream would not be easy to articulate to others—it was still vague, even to myself—and it departed radically from traditional university ways. I did not yet know how or even if I could go forward. Happily however, my colleagues, despite their considerable misgivings, agreed to let me try out my ideas and by the end of my first year back in San Diego, my dream was well on its way to becoming a reality—a small island of diversity within an almost all white university.

The Community-Based Block Program

The small island of diversity of my dream that emerged was the Community-Based Block (CBB). It was so named not only because it was to be conducted off-campus in the inner city but also because CBB students and their faculty would form an intact group (a "block" of 20 to 30 students and three faculty members) who would spend 15 to 20 hours together each week, learning from each other by working side by side as equal partners, much as I as a consultant had worked with folks during my leave. Hopefully, in time the block would become an intense and intimate "learning community."

The idea was this. Faculty would bring understanding of conventional counseling skills and theories; students would bring direct-life-experience-based understanding of differing cultural ways and world views. Special effort would be made to recruit students from as widely differing backgrounds as possible. Special emphasis would be placed on outreach and on counseling with persons who might not ordinarily come for counseling. Faculty and students would work together to figure out how best to provide services for such clients. Presumably together they would be able to provide a better learning experience than the faculty would have been able to provide alone. At the end of two semesters of work and study together, students would receive a master's degree in counseling with a specialization in cross-cultural counseling. The first CBB class was scheduled to begin in academic year 1973-74, my second year back from sabbatical leave.

Meanwhile, Back in the Classroom

During that first year while all this was being planned, my assignment was to teach two sections of a course entitled "Social and Cultural Determinants of Behavior" and to supervise our advanced students in their internship placements. Two incidents from that first year, one that took place in the classroom and one while supervising the interns merit mention in this chapter.

The subject matter of the "Social and Cultural Determinants of Behavior" course lent itself well to the collaborative faculty-student relationship that I had hoped to create. The students turned out to be receptive to my ideas, ready to experiment with sharing responsibility for their learning in the way that I proposed. The result was an informal contract between us. Together we determined what they most needed to learn and how they were to learn it. All participated actively in making suggestions for places to visit, films to see, books or articles to read, events to attend.

Recently I discovered that Henry Adams, while teaching at Harvard a century before (1871), had come up with a remarkably similar arrangement. Speaking of himself in the third person, he wrote, "He frankly acted on the rule that a teacher . . . should not pretend to teach his scholars what he did not know, but should join them in trying to find the best way of learning it. . . Since no textbooks existed, the professor refused to profess, knowing no more than his students, and the students read what they pleased and compared their results. As pedagogy, nothing could be more triumphant" [6]

One event in one of those classes that first year turned out to have special importance for me. To report it here, first I must digress briefly and put it into the context that made it so important.

The Melting Pot—Fact or Fancy?

All my early life the concept of "America as the melting pot" had seemed to me to be simply plain common sense, the natural order of things, too obvious to question. I visualized people from all nations eagerly flocking to America and within a generation or two becoming completely absorbed into the existing mix without significantly changing its basic flavor (after all, we were all just people, weren't we?). The glory of the melting pot as I thought of it was that each new group brought with it riches from its own cultural heritage. To our own Chaucer and Shakespeare and Wordsworth, as it were, the Germans added Goethe and Wagner, the Italians added Verdi and da Vinci, the Austrians Mozart, etc. The newcomers served only to enrich us, however. Their ways and views were not to have any impact on the basic nature of our existing social, political, and economic order—that was fine just as it was.

But now, in my first semester back, in a class all white except for one or two Chicanos and perhaps another person of color or two, a Chicano student brought in a guest speaker whose ideas were a direct challenge to my belief. It was one of those things that seemed trivial at the time. I have no idea how much impact our guest speaker's message may have had on the stu-

---

[6] *The Education of Henry Adams: An Autobiography,* Houghton Mifflin Company, Boston and New York, 1922, pp. 302-303.

dents in the class but I know that it started a process that in time was to have an enormous impact on me.

The speaker was Alurista, today a prominent Chicano poet but at that time one of a number of energetic and creative young Chicanos and Chicanas active in the development of a Chicano studies program at SDSU. Alurista asked, "Why haven't Chicanos melted into the melting pot like the Swedes, the Irish, the Italians? They all made it." He argued that there is a reason—that between the Chicano and the dominant Anglo culture there exist a number of irreconcilable contradictions, two mutually exclusive ways of looking at reality and that, despite being a "colonized people" (Alurista's term), somehow something of the original indigenous Chicano reality still survives. Alurista described it as "some basic indigenous core," something far more basic and important than skin color, something inherent in basic assumptions about the nature of reality and one's relationship to it."

Alurista went on to give two examples of these "irreconcilable contradictions": (1) Anglo culture is individualistic and competitive, Chicano culture is collectivist and cooperative. (Alurista claimed that indigenous Indian languages had no concept of "I," that "I," "me" and "mine" were nonexistent pronouns), and (2) the two cultures are based on entirely different ways of relating to Mother Earth. To the Anglo, the land belongs to people (private ownership, property rights, etc.). To the Chicano, people belong to the land (depend on it, are nourished by it, etc.) The relationship to Mother Earth to which Alurista referred is beautifully expressed by the Native American Indian chieftain who refused to sign a treaty giving up tribal lands, saying that he could no more think of selling the land than of selling the air above it.

Alurista's examples were not new to me. What was new was his idea that some aspects of one's culture might be so deeply ingrained that some peoples couldn't "melt" into the melting pot. The questions this raised in me were disturbing. Could what had always seemed to me to be plain common sense not be as self-evident as I had thought? Could it be that Chicanos do live, as he claimed, not just in two different cultures, but in two different realities as well—one reality the world view they share with the so-called dominant society and the other a somehow-still-surviving shadowy indigenous inner core reality? Had I gotten a glimpse of it that night in the hotel room in Austin? Had I seen it in action that weekend in Nashville? Was something similar true for Native American Indians? I remembered the sweat lodge at Rocky Boy and the conflict that had moved me so at the panel at D-QU.

Alurista presented his views to at least two or three, possibly more, of my classes during the first few semesters after my return to SDSU. His views opened my eyes to a line of questioning that was to stay with me from then on, and without which many of the important implications of much of my experience might well have passed me by unseen. (More about the influence of this on my thinking in Part Four.)

My return to the classroom that first year back home served to strengthen my conviction that I was on the right track. Once again I was learning along with my students and I could see evidence that they were learning from each other as well as from me. Student acceptance of my approach had not only been enthusiastic but few if any of them had failed to participate fully and appropriately. My return was off to a good start.

The Fourth Intern

I also learned with my interns. One incident in particular stands out. Three of the interns I supervised that first year were African-American students working at Lincoln High School in San Diego, an inner city school at that time with an almost completely segregated student body. They were assigned there for three mornings a week. This was the second semester and, since I had no morning classes, I met with the interns and told them that in order to understand what they were experiencing, I would like to do what they did and work as an intern right along with them. In addition to being their supervisor, I would like to be a fourth intern. The school staff had reservations about the idea but finally agreed that we would give it a try with an understanding that the whole idea would be dropped if at any time it wasn't working out. It worked out.

As an intern, one of the things I regularly did was to force myself to leave my office and join the commotion in the hallways during breaks between classes. Note that I say "force myself." This was the spring of 1973 and in those days I had no reason to fear physical harm. My reluctance was due to the fact that students in the hallways frequently engaged me in conversation and whenever they did, I always seemed to come out second best. For me it was a daily mini cultural plunge, and not a very pleasant one. Let me give one example to show what I mean.

In those days I often wore a medallion of some sort around my neck. Remember, the period we imprecisely refer to as "the sixties" actually lasted well into the 1970s. I had started the practice in the mid or late sixties by wearing a large leather peace symbol to show support for the anti-war protesters and then during my sabbatical years I had added Navajo silver pieces and Sioux and Hopi and other Native American Indian beadwork. On the morning I am about to describe, my medallion was Indian beadwork.

One morning when I was standing in the hallway watching the noisy march of students as they moved from classroom to classroom, one bright-eyed young man spied my neckpiece and stopped and said, "Hey, man, why don' you gimme that? My mother is an Indian." I tried to mumble some sort of reply and before I knew it there was a cluster of perhaps half a dozen students, all of whom seemed to be talking and laughing and pointing at once. They talked so fast I couldn't understand what was being said, although everyone else did. I never knew whether they were laughing at me or with me or at something else entirely. They were all so quick, so alert, so alive, so vibrant. The conversation moved so incredibly rapidly that I could only marvel at how they possibly could all understand, but clearly they all did. I was the only one who did not know what was going on. All my systems seemed to shut down. I stood there stupidly, having no idea what to do or what to say. Then the warning bell rang and as quickly as it had formed, the cluster of students vanished. I was saved by the bell.

But that is not the end of the story. Incidents very similar to this one happened to me on a number of occasions that semester. Each new time was as uncomfortable as the ones before. The reason this particular one still stands out so clearly in my memory is because of what happened next. The very kid who said his mother was an Indian, the one who had started the whole thing and in many ways seemed to be the leader of the group—this same bright kid followed me into the counseling office and sat

down with the form for planning his next semester's program and
had trouble spelling "Lincoln."

I stood there and as I watched, I understood something more
clearly than I had ever understood it before. When I was on his
turf, I was the stupid one. Now that he was on my turf—and
filling out forms and charts and budgets and all those things certainly were my turf—it was his systems that were shutting down.
Now it was his turn to be the stupid one. Never had I realized
more clearly the truth that intelligence is not only *who* you are
but also *where* you are. What would my "IQ" have turned out to
be if the test had been administered to me that day in the hallway
of Lincoln High School by one of the members of that same group
of kids—especially if the test had been one designed by a panel
of their peers! That has been one of my most important and useful guiding principles during the late years of my professional life.
Many kids who have clearly demonstrated leadership potential
on their own turf are being lost because we have not made the
classroom a turf where they feel at home. The incident reinforced
my belief in my "partnership" idea by demonstrating how important it was to a person's ability to learn that he/she have some
feeling of mutual ownership of the turf on which the learning
takes place.

CBB started in the fall of 1973, my second year back. By that
time I was permanently separated from my second wife and had
rented a small house which had a combined living/dining room
area and four bedrooms. The house was located on a back street
in City Heights in a racially mixed neighborhood on the edge of
San Diego's major barrio and ghetto areas. My house in City Heights
became the first home for the new program. The living/dining
area, furnished with borrowed bean bags and folding chairs became our classroom. The one bedroom which was off by itself
was mine; the other three became small multi-purpose group
rooms, available whenever and however they might be needed.
(Those were certainly more innocent times. No one raised questions about legal liability then—university legal departments would
clearly be seriously remiss if they failed to do so in today's more
litigious climate!)

The fall semester marked the beginning of the realization of my dream. Not to everyone is the opportunity given to translate dreams into reality. Not to many white males does the opportunity arise to become a part of a community of diversity offering quite the same level of honesty and intensity and intimacy as the one ahead for me. I have been fortunate indeed, more fortunate in fact than I had realized at first. You see, there were many things about CBB that I had completely failed to foresee—not least among them the fact that this dream into which I was about to be walking was going to become the center of my own world for the next nineteen years. I didn't know it then, but the CBB that would evolve was to change the way I would view my world for the rest of my life.

Chapter Five

Adrift as the Weed in a Great River

The great sea has sent me adrift
It moves me as the weed in a great river
Earth and the great weather move me
Have carried me away and move my inward parts with joy
—song of Uvavnuk, an Eskimo shaman

The program that got under way in 1973-74 turned out to be everything that I had hoped for and much more. Although CBB had looked at first very much like my original dream, it soon was clear that the program was taking on a life of its own. The first few years were filled with surprises as unexpected changes began to take place that were to reshape it significantly. CBB was ultimately to assume a form that would differ in many important respects from anything that I had dreamed—and, incidentally, in ways that would greatly heighten the impact that it was to have on its participants, including me personally. It was indeed as if I had been carried "as the weed in a great river" and the consequences, though unforeseen, did fill me with joy.

Recruitment

I had hoped that as many as one-third of the CBB students might be persons of color, and I had not seriously expected that we would be able to recruit more than that number. However, fourteen of the twenty-two students admitted to the first CBB class turned out to be persons of color—about 64 percent, almost twice the percentage for which I had been hoping! Aggressive recruitment of persons of color and the attractiveness of our proposed student-faculty partnership model had created a larger pool of applicants than we had expected; our selection criteria had done the rest.

Having so much greater a proportion of persons of color changed the entire dynamics of CBB into something far different—and far more powerful—than anything that I had expected. It created a turf (remember the fourth intern) on which people of color could truly feel at home, making it easier for them to feel an unfamiliar sense of ownership in an enterprise in which they had too often felt themselves to be outsiders. Anglos in the program found themselves in an unfamiliar role too—as a minority—thereby getting, as the non-Anglos were not hesitant about pointing out, some small hint of what non-Anglos commonly face in American society. And, as the non-Anglos never let me forget, I too was one of those Anglos. My years in CBB were years in a living laboratory of intense cross-cultural interactions.

A Change in Focus

My original intent had been for CBB to operate its own community counseling center which would attract clients whose problems would provide the basis for our curriculum, but we had had to abandon the idea. The very students that we wanted most were often the ones who turned out to need part-time paid employment in order to stay in school. They would not have been available to help staff such a center. So now there was to be no center. (This is why we met those first years in my house.)

My first thought had been that the practical experiences the students would obtain in part-time employment or internships at various other inner city sites could serve our curricular needs just as well. Wrong. Their experiences were being gained in such widely divergent settings that there was not enough commonality among them for the problems they were facing to be sufficiently relevant for the purposes of the group as a whole.

Before I could come up with a new solution, CBB gave me another surprise. The problem resolved itself. Or, rather, the CBB students resolved it themselves. Instead of content that emerged from problems common to tasks performed outside of CBB, in a very real sense CBB became its own curriculum. Almost immediately important "content" began to emerge spontaneously from within the group itself—to emerge out of the problems and conflicts, interpersonal and inter-group, that inevitably arose when a group of people chosen by design to be so diverse found themselves together in a pressure cooker situation where they had to arrive cooperatively at basic decisions that affected them all.

CBB was a living microcosm of the multicultural reality of the larger society with most of its attendant conflicts. In the close, long-term, intensely personal interaction of the community setting, students and faculty alike were forced to confront and deal with their own racism, sexism, ageism, elitism, homophobia, and other biases as well as with their differing cultural values and beliefs. All this was often painful. The issues we were learning about were issues in which we were personally deeply involved. By sheer good fortune, CBB became "person centered" instead of "problem centered." This turned out to be the most impactful change of all. It focused the attention of CBB students and faculty largely inward onto ourselves and onto problems we ourselves were living instead of exclusively outward onto the problems of others (clients and prospective clients). Much of the explanation for CBB's potent impact on its participants, I believe, traces directly to this fortuitous change in focus. Certainly that is true for me. This was nothing I had planned, but there I was, right in the middle of it all.

An Anglo in Diversityland

As CBB got underway another big surprise was in store for me, one that involved me personally, one that I didn't even recognize while it was first happening. I had hoped that CBB would provide a place for me to work where I would not be asked to do violence to my deeply cherished beliefs. It was clear from the beginning that CBB was achieving that goal. It was some time however before I began to realize that CBB was gradually becoming far more than just my workplace, that it was becoming the focus and center of my life. For me personally that was the biggest surprise of all.

Alice had to slide down a rabbit hole to get into Wonderland. Dorothy had to be blown by a tornado to get into Oz. Gulliver had to survive storms and wrecks on his travels through strange lands. As for me, all I had to do was to drift back to San Diego and there I was—the great river had moved me, an Anglo, into a strange new world of Diversityland. Thanks to CBB's demographics, this wonderland of cultural diversity embodied much of the diversity and the conflicts of our larger society. Thanks to its focus on our own persons, these conflicts were not remote academic conceptualizations but intense, intimate interpersonal encounters. Thanks to the boundaries defining the CBB community, there was no place to run and hide. Thanks to shared community goals, in CBB we persisted longer and exposed our true selves more openly, as many times we transcended even deeply divergent differences.

Serving as a faculty member in CBB was not a matter of the traditional 50-minute faculty performances, protected by a podium or a laboratory coat, presenting to the students only the Dave Malcolm I wanted them to see. In the CBB circle, we the faculty sat exposed, warts and all, for 15 or more hours each week, learning more about ourselves from our students while they were learning more about themselves from each other and from us. This was a far cry from my year and a half as a full-time consultant, as much as I still value that important period. Then I flew in and a few days later flew out. Intense as it was, I was involved briefly and then gone. Now I was with the same people day after day after day in deeply personal interaction. Then I was a visiting dignitary, usually treated with respect and appreciation. Now it was more like what-have-you-done-for-us-lately? Now I was in CBB, and CBB was truly a mini Diversityland.

Still More Changes

As my life became more and more involved not only with CBB itself but with CBB faculty members and former students as well, I found myself becoming less involved in many of my former activities. After two or three years with CBB, I had pretty much stopped attending conventions and was dropping some of my memberships. I no longer served on as many committees and gave up virtually all of my consulting. I do not wish to depreciate the rewards that my greater visibility during my years in the fast lane had brought me, nor the very close and valued friendships that I had made then. Still, I realize now that there had been much that was cold and remote and lonely about that life that was in marked contrast to my life in the CBB community. CBB was not all conflict and stress, though conflict and stress were often present and our dealings with them were important. CBB was also warmth and closeness and caring that transcended differences. Almost everything in life in CBB was personal; almost everything in the fast lane had been impersonal. In retrospect, it is clear that I was opting for the warmth of the personal.

These changes, like so many other important changes in my life before them, were not something that I deliberately planned. It seemed at the time, and it still seems, as if somehow they just happened. In the words of the Eskimo shaman woman's song, the great sea had certainly "sent me adrift" and I had been moved "as the weed in a great river." Fitting metaphors for my own fortuitous and joyous journey. CBB reality did indeed turn out to be everything I had dreamed for it, and much, much more!

And yet. . . In a way that is hard to put into words, I was always aware that I was both a part of, and yet not a part of, the CBB community. This was not in any way similar to my feelings those times in the hallways at Lincoln High School when I was physically present but at the same time uncomfortably aware that I hadn't a clue as to what was going on. Nor was it at all like the evening with Dusty Wilson in Texas when we felt like two waifs standing outside with our noses pressed against the windowpane watching the bright candles and warm fireplace at the party in the room inside. No, I had a clear sense of what was going on and I was very much inside the warm room and a member of the party.

And yet. . .

Maybe it was the age difference. No doubt that played a part in it. No doubt also, no matter how much I professed otherwise, at some level it was in part because I was still "the professor" both to the others and to myself. Both were important. But somehow the "and yet" was chiefly the "Anglo" that was still in me from my boyhood days in New England.

Yes, even though I certainly was very much a part of my CBB community, and an important part of it, at the same time I was not fully a part of it. Even at the end of nineteen great years of life in Diversityland, for all my changes, somewhere deep inside I still was and always would be Anglo. I wonder if this ambiguity is not at least somewhat similar to what people of color experience, no matter how long or how successfully they have been living in the white dominated world.

A Pattern of Diversity

Group photo of the San Diego State University Community-Based Block program students and faculty, academic year 1982-83. The following percentages represent the self-described ethnicity of CBB students for the first twenty years of the program: White/ European American, 31%; Chicano/ Latino/Hispanic, 29%; African-American, 24%; Filipino, 5%; Native American Indian, 3%; Asian/Pacific Islander, 3%; other (Eskimo, Lebanese), less than 0.5%; mixed (two or more ethnicities), 4%.

Chapter Six

Inside CBB

"....and the white people suddenly realize
they are in a whole new ball game,
and they are <u>not</u> the home team!"
—from a letter written by a white CBB graduate

Knowledge is mastered and skills are honed in CBB. If they weren't, CBB graduates could not have succeeded in the worlds of work and advanced graduate study to the extent that they have. But CBB is more than knowledge and skills. If it wasn't, it would never have had the impact on so many that it has had—including on me,

Describing what "inside CBB" is actually like is not as easy as it may sound. The true rich *sabor* (flavor, essence) of CBB is elusive, difficult to capture in words. Most persons in CBB, myself included, are all too familiar with the experience of trying to describe to an outsider something significant that happened in CBB, and then finally throwing their hands up in defeat, saying, "I guess you had to have been there." That has almost become a CBB mantra—a refrain we in CBB have all heard or spoken over and over again. The impact of CBB is complex and cumulative and personal and oftentimes the most important events are simply too involved or too personal to lend themselves well to the retelling. Still, in this chapter I will do the best I can to supply a few glimpses into the intense, intimate, interpersonal interactions that characterize CBB.

The Community Meeting: Confrontation and Conflict

To some, the structure of CBB may look like a recipe for disaster. Certainly (as I have said before) CBB is a microcosm of the larger society with most of its attendant conflicts. Whenever decisions are to be made in community meetings, confrontations between individuals and between groups are almost inevitable. The decision-making process often does seem to run on endlessly. Frustration is common and feelings do run high. All this does have to be transcended in order to get anything done. Confrontations and conflict become a significant part of life in CBB.

I find it difficult to explain the role that confrontation and conflict play in CBB. For all their importance they occupy a surprisingly small portion of CBB time. The level differs from year to year. Words don't capture it in action very well. Still, somehow the community-meeting decision-making process, confrontational as it often is, does seem to succeed. Topics that could be counted on to result in confrontation early become sources of in-group humor later. As need for protective pretense lessens, openness and genuine intimacy become possible.

Lessons Long Remembered

The two examples that follow capture some small sense of confrontation in CBB in action. The source of the first example is the same letter from a white graduate from which both the quotation at the beginning of this chapter and the title of this book have been taken. Here the writer recalls her first day in CBB some ten or more years before.

"I remember that first day in CBB, 35 strangers—white, Hispanic, black, a few Asian and Indian—eyeing one another—and the faculty saying 'Okay this is your program, what do you want to do with it? What do you want to do? What do you want to learn?' and a few brave souls manage to speak a few tentative answers and then someone says 'You notice only white people are talking?' and the white people suddenly realize they are in a whole new ball game—and they are NOT the home team!"

Whites are not the only ones to face confrontation in CBB as the next example shows.

It was one of the first meetings of a new CBB year. The group had decided to split up into the separate ethnic groups so each person could share his/her own personal experiences with oppression. The smallest group was the Asian and Pacific Islanders—two small, soft-spoken, shy, almost timid young Filipinas and one young Japanese woman. One sympathetic white male student volunteered to join them "to even the groups up a bit." The three gratefully accepted him into their group and then were thunderstruck when the voice of a person of color coldly asked, "You mean you are going to let a *white man* tell *you* about oppression?" Both Filipinas broke into tears at the unexpected confrontation and were unable to answer.

It was a painful moment for them, but also a significant one. All three of the young women not only survived it but by the second semester had earned the affectionate nickname as the "Filipina Mafia," a title they bore with pride. In fact, at graduation they gave me a T-shirt with the wording "DAVE—Honorary Member of the Filipina Mafia" printed on it. I still keep the much worn and now moth-eaten old thing hanging in my closet.

Recently—fifteen years later, maybe more—I talked with those same two Filipinas, both now successful young professional women active in their community affairs. Both remembered that incident vividly. In fact, both remembered the name of the Anglo male, a detail I had long since forgotten. Both also remembered how painful the incident had been for them; both remembered wondering if they wanted to come back the next day. But both also now recognized it as a cherished moment that was a turning point in their lives.

Intensity and Intimacy

"Inside CBB" is not solely a place of conflict and confrontation, it is also a place of warmth and tenderness and support. Each year in CBB there are moments of unforgettable intensity and intimacy—moments which most often are too private and too personal to describe in publication. Despite our many differences, and despite all the conflicts and confrontations between us (or, maybe because of them!), CBB students year after year openly turn to their fellows and find support in times of emotional crisis. Sometimes it has been a dying parent, or a troubled marriage, or a family member with AIDS; on other occasions it has been the loss of a friend or relative in gang warfare or some senseless drive-by shooting.

Sometimes these intense and intimate moments take place in one or another of the various small groups within CBB, sometimes they are brought up in community meetings in the presence of the entire group. Persons from all ethnic groups have shared some of their most private selves before the total group without regard for the ethnic differences between themselves and those from whom they have found support. On some occasions, students have even postponed bringing up urgent personal matters until the entire group could be present.

The openness and trust with which persons have shared and the caring and immediacy with which the group has responded in support have never failed to impress me. I remember the time when Harrison, a gay student, first came out of the closet and talked about his pain in living his life and keeping such an important part of himself secret. Even though the entire group was supportive and caring, I found myself worrying about how he—a sensitive young African-American male—might be treated if word got back to campus. I needn't have worried. I learned later that two other CBB members, two of his powerful African-American brothers, had spread the word on campus that anyone who gave Harrison a hard time would have to deal with them. Knowing those two brothers, I had no further worries.

The CBB Network

The year-long National Defense Education Act Institutes in the 1960s after which CBB had in part been modeled had produced strong bonds among students that had resulted in long-lasting friendships. I had assumed that the same would be true for CBB students as well. This time I had assumed correctly, but nonetheless once again CBB had a surprise in store for me. Below is a tale I've heard from CBBers many, many times, each time so similar as to be almost interchangeable.

The tale as it is told to me each time goes like this: "I was at a meeting (conference/workshop/etc.) in Sacramento (Fresno/ Tahoe/etc.) last week (weekend/month/etc.) and at one of the sessions there was this other person across the room from me who kept speaking up and I really liked the things she (he) had to say. So afterwards I went up to her (him) to tell her (him) that I'd liked what she (he) had said, and we got to asking, 'where did you go to school?' and stuff like that. And, I might have known, she (he) was from CBB!"

This is a level of bonding that I hadn't expected—this almost automatic and immediate bonding among graduates from different CBB years. The result has been a CBB network more powerful than anything I had anticipated. CBB itself has benefited from it—graduates from former years do much of our recruiting for us. Year after year, many of our strongest candidates have told us that they were urged to apply by some former CBB graduate, or that they had decided to apply after hearing a former graduate talk about what the program had been like. If I were asked to select the one thing that tells the most about the *sabor* of CBB, this almost magical bonding among graduates from different years might well be it. There is a saying that, "You can always tell a Harvard man. . .but you can't tell him much." Apparently you can always tell a CBB graduate, period! What's more, this bonding and networking seems to take place with utter disregard for ethnic/cultural lines.

Pressure Cooker, Si—Melting Pot, No

Although the openness and intimacy so important in CBB and the bonding and networking that characterized CBB graduates showed almost complete disregard for social, cultural, racial and ethnic divisions, CBB was no melting pot. Quite the opposite. Oxymoronic as it may seem, the same students who had learned in CBB to cut so cleanly through the barriers of cultural differences had at the same time found CBB to be a time and place for developing a stronger and clearer sense of their own cultural identities.

For many CBBers, this was a matter of rediscovering roots that they had turned their backs on. This was especially true of those apparently thoroughly acculturated second or third generation children from immigrant families whose upwardly mobile parents had striven to protect their children from their own painful personal histories. Many parents deliberately had not taught their children their original language in the hopes that they might fit more readily into mainstream American culture. Others had avoided telling their children about the humiliating aspects of their struggle as immigrants in America in order to protect them from this shame and pain. Many CBBers told the following story: when they asked, at first their parents had been reluctant to talk about the past but eventually had agreed. Once started, out came old photos and family letters and tales of hardship and struggle that the younger generation had never heard before. And along with a renewed sense of identification with and belonging to their own culture came an entirely new understanding of their parents' lives and a bonding with them at a new and deeper level.

Many of the young adults whose lives had been largely a matter of acculturation into the Anglo world discovered that deep down inside they harbored a hunger for their roots. Young Chicano males who had been going blithely through life as Peter or Ralph or Mike proudly left CBB as Pedro or Raphael or Miguel. The same students who were learning to reach across old barriers to others who were different from themselves were at the same time rediscovering and becoming more firmly grounded in their own indigenous roots. In CBB, the two clearly were not mutually exclusive.

My own years in CBB brought me a new awareness of peoples different from myself. At the same time the same process kept me constantly aware of how "white" I am. Nothing about CBB made me any less white. Nothing about my experience in CBB supports the notion of a melting pot. Instead, CBB suggests that acculturation does not have to mean turning one's back on one's roots. Cultural identification is not necessarily an either-or thing. Deep levels of identification with and appreciation of one's original culture need not preclude appreciation and adoption of elements of others, nor vice versa.

At the time that CBB celebrated the graduation of its 25th class, some members of the class designed a T-shirt in honor of the occasion. Included in the design on the back were the words, *Unity Through Diversity*, and on the front, *Lean on Me.* Each time I see that shirt and read those words I realize how well those students had captured the very point that I am trying to make here. The point of the CBB story, as these T-shirts show, is that it is through the celebration of diversity that true lean-on-me unity is developed. *E pluribus unum*, please take note.

The Essence of CBB

What is the *sabor* of CBB? All of these: the conflicts and the confrontations, the openness and the honesty, the intensity and the intimacy, the self-discovery essential to the release of personal power, the bonding across years and across ethnic lines and the spontaneous networking it produced, and above all the interpersonal interactions in a climate of trust and warmth. The total CBB experience—that's the *sabor* of CBB to me.

The unique vantage point of CBB gave me an opportunity to have intimate glimpses into the personal worlds of numerous persons from a variety of cultural/ethnic backgrounds. I grant that in many respects the CBB community was an artificial one, not the least being the high level of acculturation of the participants—all CBB students had previously completed at least four years of college. But CBB was far from artificial in one extremely important respect—its unusual degree of openness and honesty and minimal need for protective pretense. In this respect, reality in CBB was arguably more real than in most of the more natural settings in which intercultural group interactions typically take place. It was my great good fortune that I was a part of this total CBB experience.[7]

In Retrospect

Life inside CBB was the culmination of my late-in-life Anglo male odyssey into the wonderland of cultural diversity. For almost two decades most of my work and much of my personal life involved persons of color. I didn't plan it that way, I didn't intend it to be that way, and I certainly didn't expect it to turn out that way. But I am very glad that I followed the path I did, very grateful that my life has been enriched by so many experiences that I otherwise never would have had and warmed by so many friendships that I otherwise never would have made. Above all, glad because otherwise I might have missed out on so much of my own humanity.

---

[7] There is much more to the CBB story than has been included in these chapters. Readers who are interested in more information about the origins, nature, and successes of CBB or in understanding better the reasons for its impact will find more details in Appendix A, page 151.

Thanks to the '60s and my students and my own children, I did not continue along the career path that previously had seemed so logical; thanks to my sabbatical leave, my world did not continue to be virtually lily-white. Thanks to both, I dropped out of the fast lane that previously I had always simply assumed that I would follow. My father and my only brother both were successful school administrators and I truly believe, perhaps immodestly but I think realistically, that if it had not been for CBB, I might well have climbed high up in university administration. Had I done so, I might have cast a longer shadow. I might have touched many more people, but I would not have touched them so directly nor would I have been touched so deeply by them in return. And the loss would have been mine.

Life has been kind to me. I very much doubt that I would still be alive and writing this today if I had not exchanged all the pressures and stresses on my body that the fast lane would have entailed for the nourishing intimacy and warm humanity that I found inside CBB.

"Two roads diverged in a wood, and I—
I took the one less traveled by,
And that has made all the difference."
— Robert Frost, The Road Not Taken

Part III

Racism, Sexism and Affirmative Re-action

SIX MANIFESTATIONS OF RACISM

Overt

Institutionalized

Covert

RACISM

Passive/ Inadvertent

Ethnocentric

Internalized

Victim Racism

When someone is hurt, hated, feared or in any way placed at a disadvantage because of skin color or ethnicity alone.

Beneficiary Racism

When someone is helped, favored, preferred or in any way benefits because someone else is placed at a disadvantage because of skin color or ethnicity alone.

Wherever Victim Racism exists, Beneficiary Racism is automatically present, and vice versa.

Chapter Seven

The Cycle of Racism ...and Sexism, Etc.

"We have met the enemy and he is us."
—Pogo

Racism. It takes many forms, it manifests itself in many ways. It can be overt, it can be covert, it can be institutional. It can be internalized, it can be institutionalized. It can be intentional, it can be inadvertent. It can be active or it can be passive. It is so complex, so complicated, so subtle, so brazen, so elusive, so all-pervasive that its full extent is almost impossible to grasp. In fact, I am not at all sure that it is ever fully understood. Despite all the time and energy I've spent musing about it these past years, I'm certainly sure I don't understand it. Clearly this is going to be a long chapter. For openers, a few words about the history of my own racism.

"I'm Not Racist"

I am almost embarrassed to admit, even to myself, that for many years of my early adult life I used to insist that I was not racist. As a matter of fact, for a long time I had myself convinced that I *couldn't* be racist. I remember that I would argue that when I was growing up in my hometown, there were never any people of color around to be prejudiced against so naturally I never learned to be prejudiced against them. What's more, Jimmy Rosenthal was my father's personal attorney and best friend. Jimmy was Jewish and the only Jew I knew, so I never became prejudiced against Jews either. It wasn't that I was claiming any higher moral ground or anything like that. I simply believed that I had been lucky enough during my formative years not to be exposed to racism, that's all. I continued to believe this for years, until well after I had graduated from college.

Of course, I readily acknowledged that I had grown up in a world fiercely prejudiced against Democrats and Catholics and the Irish, pretty much in that order. I readily admitted that I did have to struggle against residuals of those old biases from time to time, but I claimed that for the most part they had faded away during my first few years after college, what with my marriage and my politics changing, and FDR as president and all that. Besides, these weren't racial. When it came to racial prejudice, I believed, I had been one of the fortunate ones. I had escaped. The most amazing thing about it all is that, to the best of my memory, at no time that I can recall did anyone in any way in my all-white world ever question or challenge either my logic or the facts on which I based this claim. Or perhaps it isn't so amazing at that. I certainly believed it myself. The trouble is, of course, that it wasn't true.

A World Filled with Racism

In all fairness, I should point out that my childhood world in our small village in the Deerfield River Valley was a very good place to grow up—two brothers and their dog free to roam the rural countryside from dawn to dusk, exploring the woods and fields and streams and country roads as far as their legs could carry them. Indeed, it was almost idyllic in many respects, but certainly insulation from exposure to racism was not one of them. As I look back today, I can see that it was a world filled with racism. We chanted an unexpurgated "eeney meaney miney moe, catch a nigger by the toe," spoke of "a nigger in the wood pile" (or "the chicken house"), said, "Who was your nigger servant last year?" when asked by someone to do them a favor, and in school we sang about all the "darkies" on the old plantation in the Stephen Foster songs.

"Nigger" was a favorite put-down until we were old enough to graduate to four-letter words. Actually, African-Americans came off better in some respects than most other people of color. On the radio, white comedians in blackface portrayed amiable characters such as Amos and Andy ("ow-wah, ow-wah, ow-wah") and The Two Black Crows ("I thought it wasn't what I thought it was") who, while not too bright, were family favorites and objects of a patronizing sort of affection. I knew from the movies that pickaninnies were cute and from *Uncle Tom's Cabin* that good old Uncle Tom had been loyal to the end. I even knew that the Ku Klux Klan were the bad guys and that lynching was a bad thing. And "nigger toes" (Brazil nuts) were a favorite holiday treat!

On the other hand, when we played cowboys and Indians, nobody was ever willing to be an Indian. So we all were cowboys and fired our imaginary "bang—you're dead" bullets at the rampaging hordes of rocks and trees. We knew that Indians burned villages and kidnapped kids and that the only good Indian was a dead Indian. I do not recall any mention of "noble savages" until well after I reached college. (Historical note: Moses Rice, our town's first settler, was killed by raiding Indians in a field near his home in what is now the center of our village.)

To us, all "Orientals" were Chinese. None of us ever knew one, but we all knew how cruel, sneaky and evil they were—these Dr. Fu Manchus were formidable foes, but good always won out in the end. We taunted the imaginary wicked enemy by chanting "Chinky Chinky Chinaman, belly full of rice." Mexicans were either lazy, ignorant good-for-nothings, or fierce and ruthless bandits and sometimes, inexplicably, both. And on and on. In retrospect, our little rural world was far from racism free.

The Water and the Fish

One of my favorite sayings, one that I have been using in my classes and workshops for more than thirty years, goes like this: *I don't know who it was that first discovered water, but I am sure that it wasn't a fish.* It comes to my mind now when I think back about racism and my boyhood world. Like water in the world of the fish, racism in our world was so common, so familiar, so all-pervasive, that it became invisible to us. We did not—indeed, could not—see the demeaning and insulting racist aspects in things we saw as innocent childish games, as old familiar music, as common expressions, as "humorous" or perhaps even "realistic" racial comments or anecdotes or attitudes or theatrical portrayals. Not that we actually couldn't see all those things, there was just no way we could see them as racism. Racism was something else, something abnormal and abhorrent and remote. We weren't racist.

Of course as I got older I no longer believed the more obvious factual distortions I had believed as a child, but the invisible negative racist attitudes that I had developed remained embedded deep down inside me and I remained unaware that they were there, at least for as long as my world remained almost exclusively white. Not that I was ever a really bad guy. I do not think there were many times, if any, that I ever let myself do something that I consciously knew was racist. But there was so much about racism that I didn't know. Had my childhood included more persons of color, perhaps I might have had fewer racist attitudes, perhaps more. Who knows? But not until my years in CBB would I begin to see racism in it's bigger picture.

Defining Racism

Just what is racism? "When I use a word," Humpty Dumpty said in *Through The Looking Glass,* "it means just what I choose it to mean—neither more nor less." Without realizing it, I clearly had been operating on this principle during those years when I used to argue (and believe) that I couldn't possibly be racist because in my hometown there had not been any people of color for me to learn to be prejudiced against. You see, Humpty-like, I was insisting that racism meant precisely what I had chosen it to mean, neither more nor less—and what I had chosen it to mean (with a little help from my culture) was so specific that most of what I now think of as racism was ruled out. In effect it became invisible to me. I had defined racism in such a narrow, self-serving, simplistic way that on the one hand it let me define myself out—by my definition I was not a racist—and on the other hand it permitted me blithely to ignore (define out) the world of contradictory evidence all around me.

I am not alone in adopting the Humpty principle. How else can one explain those people who seem to believe that to all intents and purposes, racism in the United States has by now become ancient history. How else explain the editorial that appeared not long ago in a presumably liberal magazine that stated, and I quote it exactly, "Thanks to Rosa Parks and Martin Luther

King, this nation is no longer a racist nation," a declaration that seemed mighty premature to most of the CBB folks I knew. Or those who protest against programs of affirmative action because, they assert, that while affirmative action may have been necessary at one time, it is necessary no longer. (More about affirmative action in the next chapter.)

In order for these people to believe what they are saying, and clearly most of them do, they must be living by an extremely narrow definition of racism. The definition of racism from which they are operating lets them limit racism mainly to KKKers and Rednecks and Skinheads and Nazis and others of their ilk. This is racism all right, and it is against the law, but those who hold the view that this is the total extent of what racism is are conveniently unconcerned about the many racist slights and slurs, direct or indirect, that are not against the law but whose cumulative effect is almost as lethal.

Their definition does two things for them. First, it excludes the "definers" themselves from among those they define as racist. Second, it leaves out so much that the true complexity of racism becomes invisible to them. In these respects the similarity of their thinking to my own thinking, when I used to believe that I wasn't racist, is so striking, it makes me cringe. It's a view that is quickly refuted by any close-up look at how the world actually works. Still, it is held by a surprisingly large number—perhaps even a majority—of whites today.

And there are other similarly overly simplistic definitions. I know of folks who maintain that "only whites can be racist." The key words, they say, are *power* and *domination*—only members of a racial group with the power to dominate members of other racial groups can be racist. In this country, they say, whites have all the power; ergo, only whites can be racist. And, since all whites benefit, if only passively, by living in a society in which racism exists, all whites are racists.

White domination over powerless members of other racial groups obviously is racism, but to limit racism in this way once again is far too narrow a definition. It ignores other well-known forms of interracial hostility such as conflict between Chicano, African-American and Asian youth gangs and the conflict in many urban communities between African-Americans and/or Latinos and Asian shopkeepers. Somehow that isn't racism. Like my own disclaimer did for me, this definition not only arbitrarily cloaks the full complexity of racism in virtual invisibility, it also conveniently excludes most of those who believe it from considering themselves as racist.

There are also those who claim that racism is simply pathology—not pathology of society but rather pathology of individuals—and that all racists are mentally sick people who need treatment. In many respects, this is an attractive idea. Certainly racism does have some of the elements of delusion and paranoia and certainly some racists are sick people who need treatment. But the proposition that all racists are sick people, and its corollary that only sick people are racist, seems to me to be of dubious value. You see, much racism is not so much individual as institutional. The pathology definition leaves that whole area out. Though more sophisticated than the other two, this definition also oversimplifies the picture so much that it tends to hinder rather than promote progress in dealing with the problem of racism.

I am reminded of the poem about the six blind men from Indostan who went to "see" the elephant. (See frontispiece.) You remember—one grasped its tail and thought the elephant was "very like a rope," one bumped up against its side and thought it was "very like a wall," and so on. There is a notable similarity between those assumptions about the elephant and the preceding definitions of racism—each of the definitions, like each of the assumptions, carries within it a substantial element of truth but still totally misses the whole picture.

Racism as Elephant

Like an elephant, racism is a many-faceted thing. I may not yet have a picture of the whole elephant, but I have seen enough to sense how complex a beast it actually is. It manifests itself in many ways. As I said at the start of this chapter, sometimes it is overt and sometimes covert, sometimes it is individual and sometimes institutional (and it can become institutionalized). It can be intentional or it can be inadvertent, active or passive, and it can be internalized. It can take either the form of preferential (or beneficiary) racism, or of hostile (or victim) racism. Racism is all of these. . .and more. Understanding the anatomy of racism is a matter of more than merely identifying a few parts, it means understanding the complex interrelationships between them all.

In a sense, racism itself is as invisible to us as the elephant was to the six blind men from Indostan. We have only the many manifestations of racism-in-action to provide us with clues to the anatomy of the beast. Much of the remainder of this chapter will be devoted to identifying and examining as many of these manifestations as possible. Or, to keep my elephant metaphor, I should say that I intend to report on as many different aspects of this racism elephant as I have been able to bump into so far.

Some Other Useful Metaphors

When I am thinking about racism, there are three other metaphors that I often find useful. (1) Racism is also very like an iceberg—only its tip is generally visible; its largest and most dangerous parts often lie invisible below the surface. Remember, the Titanic was sunk by the part below the waterline. (2) Racism is also very like a virus or a cancer—it is a destructive, virulent intruder or an ugly, malignant runaway growth that has invaded and firmly established itself within the body of the social organism. (3) Racism is also very like that mythical nine-headed creature, the Hydra (who grew two new heads whenever one of its heads was hacked off)—it manifests itself in multiple forms and, when the civil rights movement hacked off some of racism's most abusive manifestations, subtler new manifestations quickly began to emerge.

These metaphors remind me to emphasize an important point. Almost all of the things that I have to say about racism apply equally well to sexism and to homophobia and, to a lesser extent, to various other forms of prejudice against target groups. This is certainly clearly true for these metaphors. Take, for example, the "virus" metaphor. Racism, sexism and homophobia can be viewed as three strains of the same virus—the dynamics are virtually the same in all three. The gender strain is every bit as virulent (violent) as the color strain and perhaps even more intransigent (treatment-resistant). The homophobic strain is arguably the most violent of all, certainly as intransigent and reprehensible as any. This chapter, its title not withstanding, is not about racism and sexism alone.

Now for a look at the rest of my elephant, a look at the many and varied manifestations of racism as I see them.

A Working Definition of Racism

In order to talk about racism-in-action in its many and varied forms, I need first to make my own working definition of racism clear. Remember, like Humpty, when I use a word, it means just what I choose it to mean. The more I have learned about racism, the more I have become convinced that the chief problem with definitions, including the examples discussed earlier, lies in the limitations they arbitrarily create—limitations that, like groping only one part of an elephant, preclude understanding racism's full complexity. What's more, these piecemeal definitions at best lead only to piecemeal approaches to racial problems and consequently to only partial and inadequate solutions.

In order to avoid this pitfall, in writing this chapter I am using the broadest definition I can think of, to wit: "*racism is any unequal treatment, preferential or hostile, deliberate or inadvertent, active or passive, that is based on the ethnicity, color, or race of the person or persons involved.*" A similar definition, with the substitution of a few words, applies as well to sexism and to homophobia.

Racism, as I have defined it, is found in many forms. To show how complex the beast really is, I will describe, sometimes at length, some of the many ways it manifests itself as I have come to understand them. Even though my list is long, I make no claim that it is complete. Taken together, I think of this list as my description of the "anatomy" of racism, at least as far as I have been able to grasp it to this date.

Overt and Covert Racism

Overt and covert racism are two of what I think of as the three visible manifestations of racism—I think of them as visible because it seems to me they only make up the visible tip of the iceberg. They are easily observed and sufficiently familiar so I do not need to spend much time on them. Overt racism is what most of us think of first when we think of racism. In overt racism, the unequal treatment is open and deliberate. There are numerous familiar examples such as lynching, cross burning, spray painting swastikas, segregating buses and rest rooms, gay bashing or Asian bashing, white supremacy, KKK, genocide, etc. Typically the perpetrators are acting deliberately and openly, often boastfully, and acknowledge their deeds, at least to their cronies.

In covert racism, the unequal treatment is disguised or covered up or denied, usually by some form of rationalization. (Rationalization equals substituting a good reason for the true one.) A familiar example: "We would be happy to hire persons of color if we could find any who are qualified." Somehow the qualifications specified manage to screen out most people of color. In covert racism the disguising may be deliberate but sometimes the perpetrators have actually convinced themselves, and sincerely don't believe that their behavior is racist. One can be a covert racist and not even know it, but the unequal treatment that results is just as racist and hurts just as much as it would have if the perpetrator had been fully aware of the racist nature of the act.

Institutional Racism

The third of the three visible manifestations of racism is institutional racism. In institutional racism, the unequal treatment is systematically carried out in some institution as a matter of policy. Typically those responsible for institutional racism are fully aware of what they are doing and believe it to be justified as in the best interests of the institutions they represent. The classic example is the practice of "red-lining" barrio and ghetto neighborhoods by bank loan officers, and then on one pretext or another refusing to approve real estate loans on property located in districts that have been red-lined on the map.

Some systems of licensure or credentialing, especially those based heavily on tests or educational degrees, can also be examples of institutional racism. Another example, possibly apocryphal, though there is good reason to believe it to have been true: in the 1930s the seven Ivy League colleges reportedly had a gentlemen's agreement that each college would admit no more nor less than 10 percent Jewish students each year. Allegedly each agreed to admit the same quota so no one would need to take more than its share. (Small wonder so many of my Jewish friends of my generation so passionately hate the idea of quotas of any sort!)

George Lipitz describes a category he calls "contemporary" racism.[8]   Many of the examples he presents fall into the category of institutional racism. Lipitz points out that, far from being limited to the private sector, in recent decades contemporary institutional racism has permeated even presumably race-neutral liberal government programs because in practice they have turned out to be administered in such a fashion that they have actually widened rather than narrowed the racial economic gap.

Preferential and Hostile Racism

So much for the visible manifestations. But before going on to the rest of the iceberg and some manifestations of racism that, arguably, are far more significant, I want to emphasize that all racism has both its active and passive aspects. Whether racist acts are overt, covert, or institutional, they always include both preferential/beneficiary and hostile/victim aspects. Like heads and tails on a coin, the two are inseparable—they are simply the two sides of the same thing. Perhaps a more apt metaphor is the seesaw. When you push one child down (active), the other is lifted up (passive). When one group gets more than its share of the seats on the bus (active), some other group gets less (passive).

In the case of an actual seesaw, whenever one end is pushed down, immediately it is clear that the other end is boosted up. In the metaphorical seesaw of racism, this reciprocal aspect is not always as obvious. What appear to be unrelated or inadvertent consequences at the other end of the seesaw that actually are racist often pass unrecognized as such. It is easy to understand why passive beneficiaries of racism often refuse to think of themselves as passive racists. Typically they haven't done anything overtly or covertly racist themselves and don't know of anything directly or obviously racist done specifically on their behalf. Yet, even though unwittingly, they benefit all the same whenever those who might potentially have become their future competitors are being placed at a disadvantage or eliminated from future competition altogether. As I pointed out in the paragraph above, whether the victim's end of the seesaw is pushed down or the beneficiary's

---

[8] Lipitz, George. *The Possessive Investment In Whiteness.* Philadelphia: Temple University Press, 1998.

end is boosted up, the result is the same. Either way the victim is hurt just as much.

The Double Advantage

While we who are white don't usually see it as clearly as people of color do, in this society whites do have a built-in double advantage. As a group, we benefit both directly/actively from the special advantages that preferential racism may give us (*i.e.*, our end of the seesaw is boosted up) and also indirectly/passively from the special barriers that hostile racism places in the paths of non-whites who might become our potential competitors (*i.e.*, the other end of the seesaw is pushed down). People of color, in turn, face a built-in double disadvantage. As a group, the victims are disadvantaged both directly by the barriers placed in their paths and indirectly by the special advantages given to the beneficiaries (whites) with whom they have to compete. (Sexism typically gives this same double advantage to males over women!) It is not all that easy to see what a powerful advantage this passive edge actually can be unless you have been sitting on the low end of the seesaw.

We whites need to realize this in order to appreciate why so many people of color tend to see all whites at the very least as passive collaborators or inadvertent colluders in various types of racism and hence think of all whites as racist. Which, by the way, by my own definition, we all are. Starting with me. I see no way a white person in this society can fail to benefit at least to some extent from the barriers placed in the paths of non-whites, though we tend not to recognize this fact. This I believe. I don't know how many times in recent years I have thought of Robert Burns' lines in To a Louse—On Seeing One on a Lady's Bonnet at Church: "O wad some Pow'r the giftie gie us / To see oursels as others see us."

The Rest of the Iceberg

The familiar visible tip of the iceberg is only part of the story. There are also the less familiar and less readily recognized manifestations that I like to refer to as "the rest of the iceberg." On numerous occasions at workshops and in classes during the 1980s and 1990s, I have introduced this topic by playing a short excerpt from a video tape of a monologue performed by actress/comedienne Whoopi Goldberg. Goldberg is one of those unusually gifted monologists who can make a presentation so uproariously funny that persons in the audience are kept almost helplessly convulsed with laughter even while at the same time at some deeper level they remain uncomfortably aware of a soberer message beneath the surface. The excerpt I used was an excellent example of Goldberg's use of this double message approach.

This excerpt was the initial ninety seconds of a monologue in which Whoopi Goldberg is playing the role of a playful seven-year-old African-American girl who first appears on stage with a white shirt over her head, collar across her forehead, shirt and shirt tails covering her hair and hanging down her back and whose first words to her audience are, "This *(indicating the shirt)* is my luxurious blond hair." and who then goes on to share with her audience her seven-year-old's fantasies of being blond and white. The excerpt concludes with the seven-year-old saying, "And I told my mother I didn't want to be black any more. . .I did." *(The monologue continues for several minutes.)* [9]

Perhaps I wouldn't be so keenly aware of the soberer message in this skit if watching the video didn't bring back vivid memories of the pain felt by Jennifer, a young African-American mother, a CBB graduate (she and her husband were both successful young professionals with a comfortable home in an attractive neighborhood) who came to me hopelessly, helplessly in tears after her five-year old daughter had come home and tearfully asked her, "Mommy, why can't I be white?"

What is there for a mother to say?

Internalized Racism

This familiar phenomenon, also known as "internalized oppression," is one of the major forms in which racism manifests itself. Negative feelings expressed by an oppressor become internalized as feelings of inferiority by the victim until the victim gradually begins to accept the oppressor's beliefs as fact. When this happens, the victim has begun to collude with the oppressor—that is, in a very literal sense is doing the oppressor's dirty work for him or her. The experience of Jennifer's five-year-old is

---

[9] "Whoopie Goldberg," Whoop Inc., 1985.

a typical example. The fact that Whoopi Goldberg chose this theme for one of her skits is evidence that this child's experience is not an unfamiliar one among persons of color.

The form in which the expression of internalized negative racist feelings manifested itself in Whoopi's seven-year-old and by Jennifer's five-year-old, dramatic (and poignant) as it was, is actually quite common in children. Adults typically have vaguer, more generalized feelings of being stupid or unattractive or worthless, feelings which can manifest themselves in any of a number of ways, many of them demoralizing, even to the point of becoming incapacitating. Most of this begins during childhood. This internalization of racist attitudes by the victim is perhaps the most subtle, elusive, and all-pervasive of any of racism's manifestations. (Reminder: sexist and homophobic attitudes are internalized in precisely the same way that racist attitudes are—and with the very same results.)

Although the process of internalization by definition takes place within an individual, internalized racism is so widespread and so all pervasive that in some cases it actually becomes a cultural norm. Here are two examples in which the internalization of the light-to-dark skin color hierarchy has done just that.

The Skin Color Hierarchy

I have never had to worry about whether my skin color was light enough or dark enough. For two of my long-time colleagues and closest friends, it has been a very different story. Raymond was the lightest skinned member of his family. He recalls that when he was young, he was the only one who could get a haircut downtown—but the family had to drop him off a block away from the barber shop. He once told me that he had probably spent more time worrying about his skin color than any other one thing in his life. Would his fellow African-Americans think he was black enough? When whites thought he was East Indian or South American, should he let them think so?

Maria had a different problem. As a child, she was called *la prieta* (the little dark one). Even though she knew the diminutive was a mark of affection, she still was aware that the label was no compliment. Though she never had any doubts that her family sincerely loved her, there was still the lingering feeling that maybe if she had been lighter skinned she might have been that much more lovable.

In the examples above, both Raymond and Maria are getting the same messages about skin color, and in both cases it is clear that the light-to-dark hierarchical continuum is not limited to ranking the various racial groups, with the group with the lightest skin at the top and the one with the darkest at the bottom. In each of these cases, the continuum has become firmly established within a single group—a clear example of internalized racism so deeply embedded in, and so pervasive among, individuals that it has become a cultural norm that has been accepted at some very basic level by almost every member of an entire group. That the "Black Is Beautiful" movement of the sixties has in more than four decades made at best only modest inroads into this collective phenomenon is testimony to its depth and staying power.

No direct exposure to overt racist acts is necessary for the internalization of racist attitudes. Especially for children. It is very likely that Jennifer's five-year-old had had a protected childhood and had not been exposed to much if any overt racism, or even to childish teasing much beyond normal children's play. This is important. Something else other than overt racism must be involved.

Why Children Want to be White

On several occasions when I played the Whoopi Goldberg videotape at human relations workshops, 50 percent or more of the participant audiences were persons of color. Usually, immediately after the video, I asked the participants to tell me what they thought might make a seven-year-old African-American child want to be white. I have in my files one of those lists just as I copied it from the chalkboard after a workshop in 1992. Here it is:

Movies — TV — magazines — billboards — advertising (in general) — TV commercials — TV series shows — teachers — school books — Dick and Jane — history books/history — literature — language — music — humor — folklore — mythology — religion — classmates — parent's attitudes — symbolism (devil has dark skin)

There it is, unexpurgated, just as I recorded it on the chalkboard at the time. As best I can recall, this seems to me to be representative of other such lists made at similar workshops.

Note how remarkably little suggestion of acts of overt racism this list contains, though granted classmates' teasing and parents' attitudes can be mighty overt sometimes. This is all the more significant because persons of color were well represented among the participants who produced these lists. As I said earlier, something else must be operating here as well.

The list suggests that it is not necessarily any one major act or event, but more likely the cumulative effect of day-after-day, hour-after-hour bombardment by many smaller subtler everyday things, the effect of all these things together pounding and pounding away on the child. Of course, overt racist acts are incredibly hurtful and destructive. But the evidence would strongly suggest that internalization of negative racist attitudes can be accounted for without them.

One of the items that was almost always on such lists in one form or another was language. The words we use carry implications with them that are far more powerful than we usually think of them as being. After one workshop a few years ago, a participant mailed me a list of synonyms for the verb *to blacken* as an additional example of the "something else" we had been discussing. Her list motivated me to get out my Roget's thesaurus.[10]

What follows is the complete entry for the verb *to blacken*.

> blacken   verb
> 1. To cast aspersions on: blackened the good name of a great statesman. Syns: befoul, besmear, besmirch, bespatter, denigrate, dirty, smear, smudge, smut, soil, stain, sully, taint, tarnish. —Idioms: give a black eye to, throw mud on.
> 2. Dirty.

There was no entry for either "white" or "whiten." Under the adjective *black* I found six definitions, the first two neutral, the other four with heavily negative loadings:

> 1. Of the darkest achromatic visual value: a black hat. 2. Having no light: a black cave. 3. Dirty. 4. Evil. 5. Gloomy. 6. Malevolent.

Significantly, of the six, only the two neutral definitions, numbers 1 and 2, were presumed by the editors to need an example to make the meaning clear. Not a big deal in and of itself, per-

---

[10] *Roget's II, The New Thesaurus: The Expanded Edition for the 1990's,* New York, Berkley Books, 1989, p. 54.

haps, but still one more example of a deadly, destructive cumulative bombardment that never stops.

A Question Too Seldom Considered

While we are considering the impact that this "something else" has on children of color, there is a related issue, a question seldom if ever asked, but at least as important, that also needs to be considered. What is happening to white children? What is the effect of this same cumulative bombardment by "something else" on them? Everything that is on that workshop list is part of the white child's world too. The loaded language is their language too. The answer is surprisingly obvious—at least it was surprising to me until I thought about it a bit. White children, too, are internalizing these racist attitudes, only in their case the racist attitudes that are being internalized are feelings of superiority, a sense that others are "less than" they. The same constant bombardment that leads children of color to internalize racist attitudes and beliefs leads white children to internalize the same racist attitudes and beliefs, only in reverse. What becomes an attitude of inferiority when internalized by nonwhite children becomes an attitude of superiority when internalized by whites.

These racist attitudes that are internalized during childhood persist into, and are reinforced during, adult life where they eventually become a significant, though often unrecognized part of each individual's view of reality. Almost inevitably, every white child bombarded by these oppressive beliefs begins, like children of color, to accept them as simple matters of fact and, again like children of color, unwittingly to collude with the forces of oppression. No one is insulated from this process entirely. Stop for a moment to consider the enormous implications of all this for the making of a racist.

Earlier I described the experiences of my colleagues Raymond and Maria with internalized attitudes toward color that were held by people of color about themselves. The example that follows examines similar attitudes about color, this time as internalized by whites.

You Don't Look Mexican

After Maria became a young woman, well-meaning whites often told her, "You don't look Mexican," meaning that she looked more Spanish and hence almost white. She remembers that the message always hurt deeply—not only because the speakers so clearly believed that there was something inferior about being Mexican, but even more because they had unhesitatingly assumed that she did too and hence would consider such a statement to be a compliment.

Many whites claim, "I don't see color—people are all just people to me." Maria describes her personal reaction when someone says this to her as follows: "That's no compliment. It's like ignoring my gender. If, after meeting me, a person were to be asked by a third party to describe me and that person were unable to identify my gender, I would not be particularly complimented. If, in response to 'Was it a man or woman?' the person were to say 'I didn't notice; all human beings are the same to me,' the person making that response would probably not be considered to be an incredibly open, accepting, nonsexist person. But if they say, 'I don't see color,' they are clearly expecting to be considered an incredibly open, accepting, non-racist person!" (Quoted from Maria's unpublished notes.)

Many of those who read this may well be surprised by Maria's reaction. Such surprise only emphasizes how insidious internalized racism actually is. Let's face it. The very act of claiming that, "I don't see color," in this context is in itself clear evidence that the speaker has internalized the racist belief that somehow some skin colors are inferior to others; otherwise her/his "I-don't-see-color" claim would have no point. Yet the racist aspect can become so thoroughly internalized that typically the white person is genuinely confused when her/his statement is considered to be offensive. The white person, no doubt unintentionally, is sending a double message—the conciliatory message she/he presumably intends and the message with this underlying racist assumption—which, not surprisingly, most likely will be the one to which the person of color reacts.

Deeply internalized racism manages to rear its head in a myriad of unexpected ways. Note that both the white person who says, "I don't see color," and the African-American child who asks,

"Mommy, why can't I be white?" have internalized exactly the same racist message—and probably from the very same sources. Note also that both are colluding, the African-American child *with* the oppressor and the white person *as* an oppressor. Both are colluding in the perpetuation of racism. Racism can become so deeply internalized that a person literally does not know that his/her actions are racist, and hence is genuinely surprised upon receiving a deservedly hostile response. I trust that I am making my point about how incredibly complex racism-in-action becomes when you begin to examine more of the beast.

So now back to that "something else" that leads to the internalizing of racist attitudes and beliefs by white and nonwhite alike, back to the question of just what is operating here. If overt racism plays only a small role—and possibly, as I tend to believe, in many instances no role at all—just what does lie behind all those things on that chalkboard list whose cumulative effect is so powerful and so devastating. The trail leads inescapably to white ethnocentrism.

White Ethnocentrism

Whites have no monopoly on ethnocentrism of course, but it is only white ethnocentrism of which I as a white male am qualified to speak. Although ethnocentric attitudes per se are not necessarily racist, there is a powerful tendency in that direction. The Humpty Dumpty in me needed a little help from the dictionary here. Webster's Unabridged Dictionary (third edition) defines ethnocentrism as follows:

> 1. a habitual disposition to judge foreign peoples or groups by the standards and practices of one's own culture or ethnic group (this is the more usual form that ethnocentrism takes). 2. a tendency toward viewing alien cultures with disfavor and a resulting sense of inherent superiority.

Note that both of these definitions suggest racist attitudes—the second directly and the first by implication.

Anglos like me tend unquestioningly to assume that our patriarchal white western dominant culture should be the model for everyone else—that's ethnocentrism. To all intents and purposes, we simply ignore the fact that not everyone shares our same cultural values—that's ethnocentrism. Since our way of doing things has been so successful—successful in exploiting the environment, successful in exploiting other peoples—we automatically believe that everyone else would like to be like us if only they could be—that's ethnocentrism. We use those things we are particularly good at as the standard by which to judge everyone else—that's ethnocentrism. Consider the following.

The Weaker Sex

In our male-dominated society, which do we consider to be the weaker sex? Women, of course—every man knows that! What do we automatically use as our measuring stick? Size, weight, and strength, naturally. But what would we discover if we were to use endurance, longevity and ability to endure pain? That's not ethnocentrism, of course, but you get my point. And we do this for the most part without being aware that we are doing it—which *is* characteristic of ethnocentrism. (Although the dictionary definition of the word *ethnocentrism* doesn't imply it as directly, white ethnocentrism is as sexist and homophobic as it is racist; the mechanisms underlying racism and sexism and homophobia once again turn out to be virtually identical!)

We whites typically use terms like "culturally deprived" or "minority" or "disadvantaged" to describe those who are not like us. It is interesting how consistently we seem to have come up with terms that infer inferiority when what we presumably intended to be talking about is difference. Then we are surprised when others object!

Even our intended compliments are often actually slurs. A classic example is the you-don't-look-Mexican statement discussed earlier where the white speaker automatically assumes that the person of color, like Whoopi Goldberg's seven-year-old, would prefer to be white and hence feel complimented. When persons of color protest, we whites often feel hurt because they misunderstood what we meant. *They* misunderstood? Our racism can be so deeply internalized that we are completely unaware that what we are saying is racist.

I have been told that the expression, *bien educado,* aptly describes every Mexican mother's fondest wish for her children. When I first heard this, even with my limited Spanish—little more than a few such useful phrases as, *una margarita mas, por fa-*

vor—I confidently assumed that I knew precisely what the expression meant, that it meant "well educated." What's more, so too did every other Anglo with whom I have ever discussed this to this day—and so my guess is that any Anglo who is reading this paragraph now has just done so, too. And, let me add, it would never occur to any of us that we might by any chance be wrong unless and until someone else points it out to us.

We were wrong, of course. I went to the shelf of Spanish-English dictionaries in the SDSU library to look it up. *Bien educado* is defined as "well-bred, well-mannered" (American Heritage Larousse), "polite" (Harrap), "nicely behaved" (Collins). Even Humpty Dumpty, *mal educado* though he was, didn't say, "When you use a word, it means just what I choose it to mean—neither more than less." There's a lot here to muse about.

First of all, *bien educado* provides an excellent example of the difficulties in intercultural communication that ethnocentrism can create. Even a difference this obvious could go unnoticed for a long time before something awkward about the context would call attention to it—and differences are not often this obvious. Subtler differences can remain undetected indefinitely, causing misunderstandings that become virtually insurmountable. What happens, for example, in school when teacher and learner each assume different meanings (each consistent with the values of her/his own culture) for the same verbalization. However sophisticated the student's understanding may be, the exam will be graded by the teacher. Not only can it happen, it does. "Teacher, what's the correct answer to 'which is the weaker sex?'"

Second, *bien educado* is, in and of itself, a fine example of cultural differences. Not only was "well educated" (meaning schooling, degrees, credentials) one of my parents' fondest hopes for my brother and for me, but it was also one of the things most rewarded by our culture. Well-mannered is fine, but it does not help much in a culture in which the resumé is the bottom line.

For many Mexican mothers, at least in the case of their wishes for their daughters, *bien educado* may well mean not leaving home and not going away to attend the university. In a less individualistic and less competitive culture, the rewards most valued may come from relationships within one's family rather than from successes outside. As an Anglo, my own first inclination is to value successes outside. . .and yet. . .and yet. . . fast lane or CBB? . . . hmm.

Finally, *bien educado* demonstrates the kind of tunnel vision that ethnocentrism gives rise to. I am reminded again of that favorite of mine: "I don't know who it was that first discovered water but I am sure it wasn't a fish." The truly distinctive features of a culture are often so all-pervasive and familiar that they become invisible except to an outsider. Ethnocentrism is inseparably intermixed with this phenomenon. An incident that took place one weekend when I was serving as co-leader of a workshop at a local naval base provides an excellent example of what I mean.

I Never Think of Myself as White

It was a day-long training on cultural sensitivity and the workshop participants were all white, all officers or petty officers. Part way through the morning session, one of the participants protested. What he said went something like this: "You people are making too much of an issue out of race. You are the ones who are making it an issue. If people like you would just forget about color we wouldn't be having so much conflict. Look, I come here and all I hear is 'black,' 'white,' 'race' 'race,' 'race.' Why, in my normal world I never think of myself as white. I can think of a hundred other things that I'd think of myself as first. I'm a Navy officer, I'm a husband, I'm a father, I'm a boy scout leader, I'm a Methodist. . .I could go on and on and never once think to mention white. People like you are just stirring up problems where they don't exist, not solving anything."

I don't remember how my co-leader or I responded to this but somehow it was acknowledged and we went on. Not thirty minutes later, in a different context, the same officer spoke up again. "You know," he said, "whenever I come into a room and I see a black person there, the first thing I think is, 'Is he is going to hate me just because I am white?'" This from the man who never thinks of himself as white! As long as he is in his familiar all-white world, his whiteness remains invisible (and, he thought, unimportant) to him; only when he finds himself confronted by a black face does he suddenly realize how much he is aware of being white and how important his whiteness is to him. (Actually, this particular man was a person who sincerely wanted to learn. In this instance, he acknowledged his own inconsistency good-naturedly and conceded that probably he hadn't "really thought this stuff through yet." The result was, he contributed greatly to changing the attitude within the group from suspiciousness and mild hostility to openness and cooperation.)

I tell this anecdote at this point because it is not only an example of ethnocentrism itself, but also of ethnocentrism being exposed. Only when this officer was exposed to a person of ethnicity visibly different from his own was he able to "see" his own ethnocentric whiteness. There are ways in which I recognize myself in this white naval officer. My own whiteness had been equally invisible to me for much of my life. Now all that was changed. CBB was a world that rarely let me forget how white I was. That was a gift our white naval officer had never been given.

The Cycle of Racism

What does ethnocentrism have to do with internalized racism? Everything. Like a virus, ethnocentric attitudes invade and become established in the life streams of our society's institutions, becoming what I call "institutionalized racism." They permeate our entertainment, our advertising, our schools, our magazines, our television, our billboards, our humor, our language, our music—all the things that were on that workshop chalkboard list and more. And, in our good-old-boy white male ethnocentric way, for the most part we Anglos aren't even aware that it is happening.

Ethnocentrism is a key link—perhaps *the* key link—in the cycle of racism. Where does it begin and where will it end? It's a self-sustaining cycle from (1) ethnocentrism (culture) to (2) institutionalized racism (social institutions) to (3) internalized racism (individuals) and back around to (1) ethnocentrism again, and so on. It's a recurring succession of interdependent, mutually-reinforcing phenomena. If any cycle ever deserved to be called a "vicious cycle," the cycle of racism is the one. It shows no signs of being an easy cycle to interrupt. (Once again, note that the sexist and homophobic attitudes prevalent in our white ethnocentric culture become established and perpetuate themselves in our institutions and infect individuals in exactly this same cyclical way.)

The real question—and the big challenge—is: how do we break this cycle? I see myself and all whites as the products of white ethnocentrism with all of its racist attitudes. I see us all as potentially the passive perpetuators of the white ethnocentrist attitudes that perpetuate the cycle of racism. I believe that I (we) should feel personally responsible for any apathy on my (our) part that allows perpetuation of the cycle to continue unchallenged. If the cycle is to be broken, I (we) must personally become responsible for all racist behaviors of my (our) own, whether intentional or unintentional, active or passive. Only interruption of the cycle can bring significant change. Atonement may also be desirable, but in the long run it will do little to break the cycle. Apathy looks to me like the greater enemy and the more promising target.

The Case of Kristi Yamaguchi

In 1992, American skater Kristi Yamaguchi won the women's Olympic figure skating title. In the year that followed, she received far fewer endorsement offers than would normally have been expected. When advertisers were questioned about this, they insisted that they had been motivated entirely by economic concerns. When charged with institutional racism, they explained that their actions were "strictly business decisions" or "a matter of the bottom line" or even "an unfortunate fact of life"—economic, yes, but not racist.

I remember my own indignation at the time. But then, when I asked myself what I would have done differently if I had been a CEO responsible for managing a large company whose stock was being held for income by educational institutions and retirement programs or as the life savings of small private investors, I was forced to wonder. Would not I too have felt forced to capitulate and become a colluder? I saw more clearly how complex and involved the matter of racism actually is, how, directly or indirectly in one way or another, it permeates our entire social structure. The actions of the big time manufacturers and advertisers in Kristi Yamaguchi's case may or may not have been directly racist. They may instead have been only the indirect result of racist attitudes rampant in the marketplace as they claim. Direct or indirect, intentional or unintentional, the result of racism remains the same. Someone gets hurt. Someone else benefits. Racism is a zero-sum game. The cycle of racism will only be broken, if it is ever to be broken at all, by changes that reach throughout the many levels of society at large.

This I have come to believe. Racism impacts us all. It diminishes us all. Despite many cosmetic advances during my lifetime, it remains almost as pervasive, intransigent and corrupting today as ever. It is not a simple thing, and we will get nowhere if we persist in trying to deal with it simplistically. It is not simply something that you or I do or don't do, or that the KKK or a Hitler does or doesn't do, or the manufacturers or the bankers or whoever. It is more like a dangerous virus or cancer that has established itself in the body of our social system and is seriously damaging all of our social structures.

The cycle of racism is self-sustaining, deeply embedded in our past, flourishing in our present, and threatening to our future. Everyone of us who engages in, benefits from, or colludes with any practice of unequal treatment based solely on ethnicity, color, or race—and is apathetic about it—shares in the responsibility for its perpetuation. The challenge racism poses is great; the pain it imposes is greater.

"We have met the enemy and he is us." I wonder how many readers still remember Pogo, utterer of that memorable paraphrase? The message about racism that I would most like to see spread, Pogo has already expressed for me. CBB taught me not only that racism is a very resilient adversary but also that it is not only about "them," it is very much about us. It is deeply embedded within our culture, our institutions, and ourselves. It is a vicious cycle that is everybody's problem. No one of us, white or non-white, escapes untouched. I find myself feeling discouraged whenever I think of those who smugly believe that racism has already been largely legislated out of existence, or of those misguidedly would destroy affirmative action purportedly in the name of a color-fair society, or of those supercilious Orwellian dupes who have managed somehow to transform a positive term like "politically correct" into its negative opposite. These are not rednecks, they are us. Sometimes it is hard to feel optimistic.

And yet there still are moments when I almost do. . .almost. The changes I have seen in my long lifetime in many ways are for the better. Persons with darker complexions are seen in many places today that they rarely were before—on TV, on billboards, in slick magazine ads and more. Kristi Yamaguchi was getting more endorsements in 2000 than she did in 1993. When I came to San Diego State in 1953, I could walk the campus all day long and rarely if ever see a nonwhite face; on SDSU's centennial celebration day in the summer of 1997, I did walk the crowded campus for an hour or two and nearly half of the faces I saw there were nonwhite. What's more, two of the booths along the impromptu midway were sponsored by gay and lesbian campus organizations. (Their presence that day attracted no special notice, and I thought what a scandal they would have caused in 1953!) I left campus that day in a very good mood.

Undeniably, what I saw that day is evidence of changes for the better, to a very great extent thanks to affirmative action programs and to policies specifically designed to encourage various forms of political correctness, including speech codes. Political correctness, in its literal sense, means behaving (including speaking) with civility and decency and showing respect for the legitimate rights and feelings of others. I have no respect for those who have dishonestly twisted the positive expression "politically correct" into a pejorative term with which to bludgeon others into silence in order to promote their own political ends. . .and then claimed they did it in the name of freedom of speech!

I do not think I have ever heard anyone use the term "political correctness" to deride someone for espousing the Republican or the Democratic party line. This attack seems to be reserved almost entirely for race and gender and other minority group issues. Whenever someone who is trying to make this a more civil society speaks out on behalf of the legitimate feelings of "others" (meaning women and people of color, etc.), she/he is likely to be charged with a weak-kneed need to be politically correct. In a "TRB from Washington" column, Michael Kinsley summed it up.[11] "The statistic that 70 percent of American universities have speech codes of some sort, based on a survey, has now taken on a life of its own. It is grossly misleading. Most of the rules in these codes don't infringe on First Amendment values

---

[11] *The New Republic,* May 20, 1991, p. 50

in any way. In fact, they are intended to *promote* (italics in original) First Amendment values. The prototypical 'speech code' rule would be one forbidding the shouting down of another speaker."

In recent years our white society has made some progress towards modifying our attitudes towards persons who are culturally different from ourselves. Much of this progress is because so many of our formerly lily-white institutions—SDSU, for one—have made such substantial changes; many of these changes must be credited to affirmative action. If anything is going to make a meaningful intervention into the cycle of racism, it most likely will be some form of affirmative action plus an increasing concern for and sensitivity towards others. White culture still has far to go, and two of our most effective tools, affirmative action and political correctness, are both under attack, but my hope is that it is too late for those who would turn back the clock to do so. White kids watching TV or strolling the SDSU campus during the SDSU centennial in 1997 were not getting the same subliminal racist messages that their 1953 brothers and sisters did. Progress is sometimes something like rolling a great rock up a long hill. There are times when the task at hand is chiefly to keep it from rolling back down. However discouraging our task may sometimes seem, it is well worth the struggle. I know, because during my years observing the benefits of diversity in CBB, I was getting a glimpse of the rewards that could be awaiting our society at the top of the hill.

The Research Project I'll Never Do

One time when I was watching the Whoopi Goldberg tape I mentioned earlier in this chapter, an analogy came into my mind and with it an idea which I have never quite let myself abandon. It occurred to me that a young child of color is not unlike the canary a miner carries into the mine. The child is as sensitive an early detector of the poisons of racism in her/his ethnocentric environment as the canary is of the deadly gasses in a mine. At the time I had a fantasy of conducting a large-scale longitudinal study with matched samples drawn annually from each year's pool of, say, seven-year-old children of color designed to tally the frequency of their expressions of a desire to be white. The findings, I thought, might provide an objective indication of whether or not our society was making any progress toward becoming comfortable with the increasing diversity that lies ahead.

Of course, when an octogenarian contemplates a longitudinal study, it can only be in fantasy. But in the process it occurred to me that, for me at least, it wouldn't be nearly as significant to know that our courts or our employers or our legislators were becoming colorblind as it would be to learn that our teenagers were.

Chapter Eight

The Case for Affirmative ReAction

"Failure is not determined by the choices that one makes but by the lack of choices that one has."
—Nikki Giovanni

I am writing this chapter at a time when affirmative action programs are coming under harsh attack in legislative halls, at the ballot box, and in the courtrooms. This is a matter about which I hold strong personal convictions. I believe that, when you take time to look into it, affirmative action (like racism in the preceding chapter) turns out to be more complicated than some folks would have you believe. I realize that by the time this chapter is published, today's controversies may be sadly out of date. Nevertheless, I am taking this opportunity to toss my own wooden nickel's worth of opinion into the general discussion.

The material in the next few paragraphs, in a different form, was widely distributed several years ago and was reprinted in the September 13, 1995, Congressional Record.

Affirmative Action and the White Male

Affirmative action is something I know a lot about. I ought to. After all, I have benefited from it all my life. Remember, I am male, I am white, I am Anglo-Saxon and I am Protestant. We male WASPs have had a great informal system of affirmative action going for decades, maybe centuries. When it comes to preferential treatment, we are the experts. I'm not speaking only of the way our "old boy" networks help people like me get into the right colleges or get jobs or get promotions. That's important, but it's only the surface part. The affirmative action I'm talking about goes much deeper than this and is much more than just a few interventions at key moments in life. It is at work twenty-four hours a day, seven days a week, year in and year out. Because it is informal and to some extent indirect, we don't always appreciate how important and all-pervasive it really is.

However, it would ill become me to put down the old boy networks. I was admitted without difficulty to the ivy league college of my choice—it was the one my father had graduated from. (The admissions people speak of the children of alumni as "legacies," but whether this is because the college was inheriting us as students or because the college hoped to inherit money from our families, I was never sure.)

I got a teaching job right out of college in the heart of the depression—my father was a school superintendent well liked among his colleagues. Later, when I became a university professor, I received promotion and tenure in minimum time, noticeably more quickly than similarly qualified women colleagues. You see, the decision-makers knew me better—I was part of their monthly poker group and played golf with them every Friday afternoon.

Yes, the old boy network system of affirmative action has treated me well all my life, there is no question about that. Of course, nobody ever called it "affirmative action." But that is what it was—and is. Affirmative action for white males. Women and persons of color need not apply.

Indirect Impact

Impactful as the old boy networks have been on my life, however, there is another aspect of white male affirmative action that has had even greater impact. There is a flip side, a darker side which turns out to be the more influential side. Though its benefits are subtler and less immediately visible, I and virtually all other white males benefit from it practically from birth. It is constantly at work on our behalf, whether we are aware of it or not. The flip side of preferential treatment that bestows special advantages on us as white males is negative treatment that places women and people of color at a disadvantage. It's the seesaw metaphor again—the end result is the same whether our end is boosted up or their end is pushed down. When the other end is pushed down, the impact on us may be indirect, but we benefit from it all the same. We benefit as a result of what doesn't happen to us—as a result of the destructive, painful stuff that we white males do not have to endure that so many other folks face simply because of their gender or color. More later about how (and what) we whites gain because of the negative things that happen to others; first, a few examples of the sort of negative experiences that I have in mind.

The Negative Flip Side

I live in San Diego and, of the dozens of times I have crossed the Mexican border, the one and only time I was ever pulled over and had my car searched was when I had two African-American males as passengers. When I asked an inspector how long this was likely to take (I had an appointment at home), I was told curtly and rudely, "As long as it takes. Now, get back over there and wait." I felt mistreated and insulted and infuriated and I started to say so but my passengers—one a faculty colleague and the other a graduate student—calmed me, assuring me that this sort of thing frequently happened to them. So I took their advice and kept my mouth shut, forcing myself to keep a grin on my face (sound familiar?) as I tried to smother the anger churning around furiously inside me. (I probably shuffled a bit, too. I don't remember.)

Years later my car was searched at the border for the only other time in my life, this time returning from Canada. Again I had a passenger—a former student, much younger than myself, female and African-American. Again the inspectors were curt to the point of rudeness. Coincidence?

More Examples

Very early in life I knew that boys were more important than girls—and I bet that most other white males did, too. What's more, so did the girls. The messages they and we got may not always have been direct but just the same they came through loud and clear. I am reminded of the story about the guy who had sex-change surgery. When he was asked if it hadn't hurt terribly when they cut his penis, he replied, "No, not really," and when he was asked about when they cut his testicles, he replied, "Not as much as you'd think," and then he added, "What really hurt, though, was when they cut my paycheck." Painful messages are not always indirect nor are they confined to early childhood. Sometimes they can be mighty direct and they never stop coming. Ask most any woman.

Most white males like me have not had to endure those "what-is-he-doing-here?" looks any time we walk alone in a residential suburban area. We have not had to notice white women clutching their purses more tightly when they meet us walking along the street. We never have seen the "For Rent" or "For Sale" signs figuratively if not literally snatched out of the window as we walked up to the front door. And I can barely begin to imagine the bombardment by insults, large and small, that sends a five- or six-year-old running tearfully home to ask Mommy or Daddy, "Why can't I be white?" or the crippling scar this must leave on the child and the parents. People like me never have to endure the pain of having our kids come home crying and asking this question. Only quite late in my life did I discover how frequently young black and brown parents do have to live with this pain.

The late tennis great Arthur Ashe has been quoted in *Sports Illustrated* as having said that handling AIDS paled next to the pain of growing up black in America. That just about says it all.

The White Male Competitive Edge

We white males who are professional persons do not have to carry the extra burden of knowing that the slightest mispronunciation or grammatical error or any other fault or slip-up on our part can and will be seized upon by some people as validation of their negative stereotypes, not only about us but also about all people like us. Professionals who are persons of color and, to some extent, women, regularly do. (Ever hear anyone say, "Well, what would you expect from a _____?" You fill in the blank.)

We males are not constantly bombarded by negative messages about our color or gender until we begin to internalize them, to halfway suspect they may in part be true. We have not had to try to participate in class or perform at work, all the while holding this particular mixture of frustration and anger and hurt tightly inside lest it explode into uncontrollable rage. But entire populations of our potential competitors—women and people of color—have labored and still are laboring under disadvantages of this very sort as they compete with us. The cumulative competitive edge we white males get from all this may well be the most effective affirmative action of all.

Let's face it, as a group white males benefit because women and non-whites are confronted throughout life by heartbreakingly destructive negative experiences (remember the preceding chapter; remember the quote from Arthur Ashe) that have been and continue to be remarkably effective at crippling or eliminating many of those who might have been our competitors. Of course there are some people of color and women who, despite our head start, do match or surpass me and many of my fellow white males. But the facts are that we white males never really have had to compete with women or people of color on a level playing field. Few of us would have gotten to where we are today—at least not so easily—if we had not been born white and male. Think about it, think how much harder it would have been for any of us if we had been born woman or person of color. We might still have made it, but then again. . . That's something we white males don't think about often enough.

One would think that a situation so blatantly unfair, with inequities so clearly based solely on gender and/or race, would not be tolerated in our self-proclaimed "free" society, but for much of my lifetime it was not only tolerated, it never even seemed to be questioned. For a variety of reasons, a silent majority—women and persons of color—remained silent, somehow managing to grin and bear it. The silent *minority* saw no reason not to remain silent and grin and enjoy their white male advantage. Then, some four or five decades ago, the silence was broken by the civil rights and the women's movements and in the era that followed some dramatic changes have occurred. (In fairness, I acknowledge that many white males participated as full partners in this movement for change.)

The response to these voices was the advent of an equal opportunity policy which spawned a variety of programs designed to intervene in many areas, among them hiring and firing in the workplace, the awarding of government contracts, and college and university admissions. These programs we now know as affirmative action programs. Since they were created to close the gaps that had resulted from white male preferential treatment (affirmative action for whites, that is) they were actually not created as affirmative action per se, but as a "reaction" against the affirmative action that we white males had been enjoying for so long. That is what they really are and that is what they really should be known as, and it would clear the air a lot if they could be known by some label that kept this mind. However, too many other Humpty Dumpties have gone before me and now it is too late to change the name so, conformist that I sometimes am, I reluctantly climb aboard their band wagon. (George Orwell would have been amused!)

So today we have two affirmative actions—one of them clearly labeled (though mislabeled) as affirmative action, the other one clearly affirmative action though not so labeled. The affirmative action under attack today is the mislabeled one, the one that should be called affirmative "reaction," the so-called affirmative action programs that were created to counterbalance (remember the seesaw) inequities. The truth is, the attack on them that we are seeing today is, with only a few exceptions, the white male establishment fighting to regain and retain its traditional advantages.

The Attack on Affirmative Action

Admittedly, these formal so-called affirmative action programs are specifically designed to provide preferential treatment for women and people of color and, by my own definition, if gender and color were the sole basis as at first glance they seem to be, that clearly would make them racist. Taken alone and out of context, this does seem to be true. But that is only part of the picture. It's the blind men and the elephant again. Affirmative action programs exist in a context—they exist only as a part of the larger beast—and in that broader context it is the persisting inequity, not gender or color, that is the reason for the preferential treatment.

Too many people today fail to understand (or deliberately choose to ignore) the larger picture and would terminate all the so-called affirmative action programs, thereby ending these efforts to bring the seesaw back nearer to level and thus allowing the more pervasive white male preferential treatment to resume virtually as it always used to be. If they are really concerned about equity, they are attacking the wrong foe. The true foe is white male affirmative action; if it could be ended, none of the new formal "preference" programs would any longer be necessary. Unfortunately, as I write today, affirmative action for white males (the persisting source of the inequities) remains alive and well, thank you, and unthreatened by court decisions or ballot initiatives or ambitious governors. (I wish I could say the same about affirmative reaction!)

To me, the promise of America is a society which is color-and-gender-fair, not color-and-gender-blind, not as long as "blind" means blind to existing inequities that are based on color and/or gender alone. Formal affirmative action programs, despite some unavoidable negatives, do serve at least two important purposes. They make our badly tilted playing fields a little bit more level and at the same time they remind us that we still have far to go. Though they may need improving, they must be preserved. It is no solution for society to trash its current formal efforts to make opportunity a little more equal as long as so many powerful informal barriers to equality of opportunity still persist. It was President Clinton who said, "Mend it, don't end it." I totally agree, though I'd probably add, "Explain it and retain it."

Other Opinions

Not everyone agrees with me on all this, of course. There are many who hold quite different opinions. This chapter would not be complete without some recognition of them.

Justice and the White Male

The criticism that I hear most frequently about affirmative action is (1) that it is contrary to the values of a purportedly color-fair society because (2) it gives preferential treatment to women and/or persons of color and that this is unfair to white males. Only at a very superficial first glance does such an argument appear to contain any element of logic or truth. The truth is, as I have pointed out earlier, that in terms of the larger picture, far from being unfair or contrary to the values of a color-fair society, some limited amount of preferential treatment, hopefully on a temporary basis, is crucial to the cause of fairness and equity and to the defense of these values, and is clearly the lesser of evils in light of the realities of the status quo. What's more, in today's world, such preferences are often not actually as "unfair" as many whites persist in thinking; there are qualifications such as understanding of and access to an increasingly diverse society that persons of color or women often can and do bring to an institution or organization that few if any whites males can bring.

I grant that I probably would not have found any of these arguments to be very convincing when I was a young white male fresh out of school, looking for a job. I am aware that it is asking a great deal to ask anyone to suppress his/her individual interests for the good of some larger picture. I admit that I have no painless answer and yet I have no choice but to stick with the best one I have. I wish I could offer something more substantial than sympathy.

A Look at Test Scores

On the other hand, I have no sympathy for the frequently heard complaints from white male applicants for college admission who are turned down despite having test scores higher than some of the persons of color who do get admitted; they often complain that because of affirmative action a person of color was given the slot that they believe was rightfully theirs. For those inclined to indulge in this "rightfully mine" talk based upon this almost mythic belief in the infallibility of test scores, I recommend the following letter to the editor from one Jeffery Ewener of Toronto: "Any intelligence test on which high scores can be achieved by people capable of believing in anything so preposterous as the efficacy of intelligence tests is obviously fundamentally and irremediably flawed." [12]

Test scores are fallible predictors even under the best of circumstances. When used to make comparisons between persons from different backgrounds, they become especially suspect. The classic (possibly apocryphal) example is the question reported to have been used on a public school achievement test in the 1920s that asked, "In what season do the robins return?" All the kids in New England got it right but all the kids in the Carolinas got it wrong. Whether apocryphal or not, it illustrates the sort

---

[12] *New York Times Review of Books,* November 13, 1994.

of thing that can and does go wrong. My "weaker sex" question in the previous chapter may be sufficiently obvious that it could never happen, but it does demonstrate the possibilities. There is no possible way to score these questions that is fair to both regions or both sexes—you just don't give the same questions to both groups! (Let me remind you also of my own experiences with the students at Lincoln High school and my estimate of my own "IQ" when I was on their turf.)

At one point in my life, my special area of expertise was mental measurements. I taught graduate courses in that area for more than thirty years. I know how limited the legitimate uses for test scores are. Except for scores that are extremely high or extremely low, test scores alone do not predict success in college for any one individual much better than a roll of the dice. My experience in CBB bears this out. CBB students with grade point averages and/or Graduate Record Examination (GRE) scores so low that waivers were required for their admission to graduate study were consistently highly successful later in both CBB and non-CBB classes and in more advanced graduate study at other universities and/or on the job.

In one instance (also mentioned in Appendix A), five CBB graduates were highly praised as "five smart students of color" by their professor when they took his graduate course in Research Methodology and Statistics. When I checked I found that they had had the following GRE scores (Verbal + Quantitative): 930, 880, 730, 540, 470. The cut-off score for admission to graduate study at SDSU was 950; our department had been required to submit formal written requests for waiver of deficiency for all of them except the student with the 930 score. There was nothing in their instructor's assessment of their performance to suggest that any one of them had been "given a slot that rightfully belonged" to someone else with more respectable GRE scores!

The problem of culture (and gender) bias in testing has never been fully resolved. That a test is equally fair to persons coming from different backgrounds can rarely if ever be adequately established. A difference of a few, or even more than a few, points on a test score between a white male applicant's score and that of a person of color is by no means evidence that the opening was "rightfully his." Tests can be helpful when used in conjunction with other sources of data, but *always* be skeptical about decisions made on the basis of test scores alone.

A Kind Word for Quotas

Another frequent criticism is that, no matter what lengths they may go to to disguise it, affirmative action programs almost always involve quotas. For many, the q-word is not something to be spoken aloud in polite society. But quotas are not necessarily bad. (Quota is actually a term for a perfectly neutral, mathematical construct.) At the risk of sounding like a front man for the American Rifle Association, I insist that quotas, per se, do no harm; it is only persons who misuse them who do harm. Ordinarily, I am sympathetic toward those for whom history has made quota a word that carries many painful memories, but when their history leads them to oppose quotas under any and all circumstances, it is time for me to demur. Flexible quotas play a legitimate role when any organization—whether it is a business or an affirmative action program—is setting its goals. Many, perhaps all affirmative action programs have had goals that implied quotas of some sort, whether specifically identified as such or not.

A great change has been taking place in the past few decades. Persons with darker complexions are being seen in large numbers today in many places where they were rarely seen at all before. Most of the change in the workplace and on school and university campuses is directly attributable to affirmative action programs. Entertainment (movies, TV, etc.) and business (TV commercials, billboards, advertising in general) and magazines and music and many other areas also reflect the same change—thanks in part to affirmative action and in part to increasing public concern for political correctness (in its positive sense).

Children growing up today are getting a very different message about race and gender from the world around them than they would have gotten 25 to 30 years earlier. The more visible people of color become, the less likely today's white children are to perpetuate traditional ethnocentric attitudes. As I said in the previous chapter, this is the one slim glimmer of hope that I see for the disruption of the cycle of racism. I do not want to see this hope torpedoed by distaste, however understandable, for the term *quota*.

Making Things Worse

A number of voices are being raised, insisting that affirmative action programs are making things worse, not better. This is most frequently heard at the level of the professions, especially in academe, and management. The claim is that affirmative action is leading whites to believe that all people of color in the professions and/or management are at the level they are only because of their skin color, not because of their merit; that this is creating greater divisiveness between the races; and that it is perpetuating the tendency of people of color to think of themselves as helpless victims, thus creating a feeling of dependency which destroys their confidence in their ability to succeed by themselves. Many of the articulate spokespersons for these claims themselves are persons of color.

As a white male, obviously I have never "walked the Black walk" in academe and hence I am in a poor position to doubt or dispute their experiences. But I have "walked the white walk" and my personal observation of the reactions of my white colleagues is something about which I can speak, and my observations in these matters differ markedly from theirs. Granted, there are whites who seem automatically to doubt the competence of virtually every person of color. For what it may or may not be worth, my observation is that these persons represent only a small though vocal minority. The racism they are displaying is not something newly created by affirmative action programs; rather it is the surfacing of racist attitudes that they have held all along that they now express more freely because they can cloak them in the respectability of dedication to a colorblind society. I see no evidence that affirmative action is divisive; on the contrary, I am hearing a significantly increasing percentage of my white colleagues, sometimes much to their own surprise, expressing new respect for persons of color now that they have more opportunity to work directly with them.

Perpetuating Dependency

While I cannot comment from direct experience regarding whether or not affirmative action serves to perpetuate a damaging "victim complex" in persons of color, I can comment on the accompanying charge that it is well meaning white liberals like me who are unwittingly causing this perpetuation of dependency. At the risk of sounding defensive, let me state that I feel strongly that it is not necessarily falling into the trap of seeing people of color as victims to acknowledge that there are forces in society that can overpower the individual. As Nikki Giovanni has said, "Failure is not determined by the choices that one makes but by the lack of choices that one has." To me, affirmative action does not imply lending a helping hand to poor helpless victims; instead it means opening doors more widely that have too long been kept almost completely closed, it means making more choices available to folks who have had too few choices open to them in the past. A prime model: Colin Powell.

George Lipitz (whom I quoted in an earlier chapter) neatly skewers the Ward Connerlys and the Thomas Sowells and the Clarence Thomases and those other professionals who are persons of color themselves and who would end affirmative action because, they claim, it perpetuates feelings of inadequacy and lack of self-confidence in those who benefit from it. In response, Lipitiz wonders "how. . . (white professionals). . . must feel, those who inherited money from their parents, got their jobs through family connections or prep school contacts, who enjoyed the benefits of a healthy environment or a decent education because of their favored position in a discriminatory housing market." (Lipitz, op. cit.., p. 222.) Unless and until there can be assurance of an end to informal "affirmative action" for whites, those who are calling for an end to affirmative reaction programs for people of color are advocating a totally untenable position.

A Bizarre Mutation?

Many of these prominent and successful persons of color who now would end affirmative action actually benefited from affirmative action programs themselves; now they would close these newly opening doors to others. Their reasoning, purportedly, is that it is in the interest of a colorblind society. It seems to me, however, that most likely it is in large part because they have convinced themselves that as long as affirmative action programs exist, their white colleagues will never believe that they or any other persons of color actually made it on their own merit, that if there were no affirmative action programs, no one could doubt that people like themselves had made it on their own merits, and that then the persons who really count (the white power structure!) would no longer have doubts but would recognize and applaud them for what they have accomplished. In the previous chapter I have written about internalized racism metaphorically as a virus. It is hard for me not to think of this as simply a particularly bizarre mutation of the virus of internalized racism.

The Issue of Constitutionality

I am not a legal scholar and not versed in all the intricate issues involved in the constitutionality of affirmative action. I am aware that any preferential treatment based solely on race or color or gender is likely to be ruled unconstitutional, at least in those situations which involve taxpayers' money. I do not know if a legal distinction can be made between actions which are solely preferential and ones which are primarily for equalizing purposes and consequently are only incidentally preferential. By chance, however, in a book on North American Indians I did discover a reference to a situation in which the courts did uphold preferential hiring based on race: "In 1974, in Morton v. Mancari, the Supreme Court upheld the right of the Bureau of Indian Affairs to adopt a policy of preferential hiring of Indians. Such favorable treatment was not 'racial discrimination,' the justices ruled, but rather constituted 'an employment criterion reasonably designed to further the cause of Indian self-government and to make the B. I. A. more responsive to the needs of its constituent groups'." [13]

Perhaps a little reframing is in order. Perhaps careful wording could establish that in the case of affirmative action, ethnicity and/or gender should themselves be ruled a reasonable employment (or admissions) criterion. Perhaps the legal system will look at affirmative action in terms of the larger picture.

The Anatomy of a Metaphor

What about racism as a virus, affirmative action as a vaccine? The more I think about it, the more apt this double metaphor seems. The racism virus isn't a virus that invades a human organ-

---

[13] Viola, Herman J. *After Columbus: The Smithsonian Chronicle of the North American Indians.* Smithsonian Books, Washington, D. C., 1990, p. 253.

ism, it's a virus that invades a social organism. It has its own life cycle. (Do viruses actually have life cycles? I'm not sure. Anyway, this metaphoric one does.) It is spawned in the ethnocentrism of the dominant white society, it invades most of that society's institutions (schools, media, business, entertainment, etc.) from which point of vantage it infects the next generation of human individuals who grow up with the same racist attitudes and become the dominant society whose ethnocentrism perpetuates the cycle, etc.

Affirmative action, like a vaccine, is composed of small, controlled dosages of a weakened form of the racism (preferential treatment) virus. This vaccine is artificially injected into the social institutions of the dominant society, thereby producing visible changes in the chemistry (complexions) of these institutions. This, hopefully, will help to develop immunity to the ravages of racism (i.e., change the attitudes that individuals develop by modifying how they experience the world around them) and that in turn, again hopefully, in time will modify white ethnocentrism sufficiently to interrupt the cycle of racism. Sounds like it's worth a try.

Not too bad a metaphor, at that. You know, it wouldn't be a bad thing if more people did come to think of affirmative action as a vaccine against racism. . .which, metaphorically, it is. It sure would put an end to a lot of the nonsense about affirmative action that is being taken seriously today. Remember, someone has said that "People who think it is a level playing field usually have box seats." (Anon.)

Part IV

Culture, Diversity and Anglo Male Reality

Chapter Nine

About Culture and Reality

"Common sense" is that which tells us
that the world is flat.
—source unknown

This marks the end of my discussion of racism and affirmative action, both of them topics about which I hold strong personal convictions. I turn now to subtler and more elusive topics and to issues about which it is not possible to speak with the same level of conviction, but which arguably may be even more fundamental. The remaining chapters tell where my musings have led me as I grapple with ideas about the nature of culture, diversity and my own Anglo male reality.

Before I turn to my topic, another word or two about musing. Sometimes musing is something like trying to read an inkblot while knowing that some unexpected new droplet may fall at any moment and change the blot's entire shape. What's more, when musing I can never be certain how much is the inkblot and how much is my projection onto it. How does one check the reality behind a concept like *culture?* What I am trying to say is that I am very much aware that my musings, particularly in this next chapter, are sometimes little more than hunches or half-complete thoughts that I believe just might be important. Like prices in a mail order catalog, many of them are subject to change without notice. I haven't tested them. I can't prove them. The best I can claim for them is the law of parsimony—they help me account for a lot of things otherwise much harder to explain. For this reason I do take them seriously enough to be willing to go public with them. But I am aware that I am wandering into particularly deep waters when I share my musings about concepts like culture and reality. Yet the relationship between culture and reality is precisely what this chapter is all about. So, with the caveat above, I plunge full speed ahead.

Culture and Personality

At one point in my doctoral study, I enrolled in an advanced graduate seminar in Anthropology entitled, "Personality and Culture." The professor began the first session the way, so I was told, that he always did—with a slightly sexist, slightly elitist joke that was his one and only attempt at humor for the semester. As I remember it, he said something like this: "Most of the young women who register for this seminar never show up for the second meeting—they discover at the first meeting that this is not a seminar you take 'to improve your personality' and 'to get culture.'" All the male graduate students (including me) smirked appreciatively. But maybe the joke was on us.

Terminology involving race, culture, ethnicity, etc., turns out to be a tricky business. Former Harvard President A. Lawrence Lowell said it well years ago. Speaking about the difficulty of discussing culture, he said, ". . .nothing in the world (is) more elusive. . .An attempt to encompass its meaning in words is like trying to seize the air in the hand, when one finds that it is everywhere except within one's grasp."[14] The result has been Humpty-Dumptyism at its wildest. The same authors who quoted Lowell reported that they had found "over 164 definitions of 'culture'" and, in a footnote on the same page, they added "Actually, if additional definitions in Part III, in footnotes, and in quotations throughout the monograph are counted, there are probably closer to three hundred 'definitions' in these pages." [15]

Newsweek in 1995 reported that Americans used a write-in blank on the (1990) census form to identify nearly 300 "races." Such a Humpty-Dumpty wonderland babel of multi-meanings suggests that maybe the Northwestern University coeds weren't the only ones who were confused.

---

[14] Quoted in Kroeber, A. L. and Kluckholm, C., *Culture: A critical review of concepts and definitions.* New York. Vintage Books, 1966, p. 7.
[15] Ibid, page 29.

Questions About Culture and Reality

This confusing profusion of meanings was only one of the difficulties confronting me when I began confronting questions about culture and reality. Even more of a problem was Margaret Mead's lament that opportunity for true comparative study of cultures had ended in the 1950s when the transistor radio was born because, in her words (at least as I remember them) "On every isolated beach on every South Sea island, every little native kid now walks along holding a transistor radio to his ear." (See Appendix A for more.) Still, I continued to be both intrigued and disturbed by the view Alurista had expressed in my classes (chapter four) that there is some elusive basic indigenous Chicano cultural core which results in "irreconcilable contradictions, two mutually exclusive ways of looking at reality" that make it impossible for Chicanos to truly melt into the melting pot.

Alurista's views had raised this question for me: was it actually possible for two different cultures to develop two different ways of looking at something as universal as reality? The dilemma I faced: how could I ever check the validity of Alurista's assertions in view of the obvious truth to Margaret Mead's observation? How could I ever obtain the comparative data necessary to determine the truth about differences between Chicanos and Anglos when every Chicano I had ever seen or was ever likely to see (including Alurista himself) was to greater or lesser extent already "acculturated" by the impact of the Anglo world?

The answer eventually became obvious. In lieu of true comparative culture studies, I would have to rely on whatever hints and clues I could glean from whatever sources I might find. I began to look to see if there was evidence that I had overlooked before, simply because I hadn't been looking for it. Once I began looking, I discovered a number of bits of evidence which on closer inspection unexpectedly turned out to have relevance that I had not previously noticed. One such unrecognized source was an event that had taken place back in 1968. Here is the story.

A Night to Remember

My oldest daughter was home from college for the Christmas holidays and she and her then current hometown boy friend decided that the time had come to teach me how to smoke pot. This, remember, was the 1960s and I had agreed, but not without considerable trepidation. After all, I was of the generation that had believed that if you could even spell *marijuana*, you were practically a dope fiend. At the same time, I did not want to appear to be a poor sport. So it happened that one evening we were all sitting around the kitchen table and I watched intently as they rolled and twisted up the ends of a scrawny pretense for a cigarette.

Their instructions to me were simple and clear. "Inhale as deeply as possible and hold it as long as you can." They each demonstrated the process and then handed the limp thing to me. As a former two-pack-a-day man, I already knew how to inhale. I did. . .deeply. . .and held it as long as I could. . .and nothing happened. We repeated the ritual two or three more times. . .still nothing. As I exhaled the last time, I reported in a somewhat squeaky voice, "Nothing is happening."

My remark was greeted by an outburst of giggling on the part of my supposed-to-be-mentors, a response that seemed to me both inappropriate and not particularly helpful. It did not make things any better when Bonnie said to her friend, "We should have known the old man would be too uptight to get any effect." I felt a twinge of disappointment but this was quickly overridden by a feeling of pride as I realized that the truth must be that I had just too much willpower to succumb to the effects of even so powerful a drug as marijuana. It was with mixed but predominantly gratifying feelings that a few minutes later I excused myself and went to bed.

Now at this point I need to explain that the house I was then living in was equipped with one of those built-in AM/FM transistor intercom systems that pipes music from a radio in the kitchen to a speaker in the master bedroom. So, as I was lying there in bed, it gradually dawned on me that a most remarkable thing was taking place. Bonnie, whose bedroom was directly below mine, had turned on her record player—as usual, much too loudly—and not only was it playing the same recording as the radio on the intercom but, unbelievably, the two were in perfect synchronization. I lay there marveling, wondering what the odds were against the occurrence of such an incredible coincidence and then,

a few moments later, the recording ended and a new one started
. . .and it was happening again! I could hardly believe my ears.
I sat upright in bed.

Only then did I realize the truth. The music was not coming
from Bonnie's room at all—only from the intercom speaker. Out
of that usually tinny-sounding little squawk box, music was now
pouring that filled the room, bouncing off the ceiling, the floor,
the walls. I was hearing music like never in my memory had I
ever heard music before. (Although I wear hearing aids today, at
that time more than thirty years ago my hearing acuity tested in
the high normal range.) That night I had learned something about
marijuana. That was 1968. It would be several years before I realized that I had also learned something else from the experience,
something that tended to lend credence to Alurista's point of view.

Perception and Reality

I had long known that many years before, Harvard psychologist William James had suggested that each infant is greeted at
birth by "one big blooming buzzing Confusion" (capitalization in
the original) and that one of the first tasks each newly-born
nervous system faces is to learn somehow to screen out much of
this torrent of input in order to focus on what is left.[16] This had
always seemed to me to be a very reasonable and useful way of
conceptualizing it. It made me think of the analogy of a radio
tuner. Out of the myriad of wave lengths in the environment, the
tuner, in order to tune in one particular frequency clearly, must at
the same time screen out all the rest. Like the air waves, the world
our nervous systems operate in is full of clutter; we have to screen
out some things in order to make sense of the rest.

At about the same time as my introduction to marijuana, I
had heard Robert Lynch, a prominent La Jolla psychiatrist, who in
1968 was one of the few persons in the United States still autho-
rized to conduct research on LSD with human subjects, report
that his experiments were suggesting to him that what LSD actually seemed to be doing was somehow, in his words, "inhibiting
the inhibitors" so that, when his subjects were on a so-called "LSD

---

[16] James, William. *Psychology: Briefer Course*, Harvard University Press,
Cambridge, 1981, p. 21.

trip," the LSD made it possible for them to access aspects of the blooming, buzzing confusion that had been there all the time but which their nervous systems normally had been programmed to screen out.[17]

Thus James, with an assist from Lynch, had given me a plausible explanation for my experience with marijuana. It did seem possible that somehow the marijuana had temporarily given me access to music which usually my nervous system would have screened out. I already had accepted James' view that, as a matter of necessity, much of the clutter out there in my world had to be screened out in order for me to make any sense out of my world. I had always considered it simply to be a good riddance. After my experience with marijuana and music, I sometimes found myself wondering what else might be out there that I was screening out. What might I be missing? Once something was screened out, was it gone forever? At the time I found it all interesting, but it had not seemed to me to be of any particular practical importance.

All this took on new significance, however, once I began to ponder Alurista's arguments. If it was possible that the nervous system does learn to screen out certain input in order to focus on other input, as James had asserted, was it not also possible that people in different cultures might learn to screen out different things, possibly even things different enough to account for Alurista's "irreconcilable contradictions?" I did not (and do not) know enough about neurology to know if there is any evidence suggesting a physiological basis for the existence of a screening process of this sort. But physiological basis or not, it remains a useful metaphor for thinking and communicating about phenomena such as my marijuana experience and, what's more important here, it encouraged me to continue to explore the possibility that there could be some credible basis for Alurista's views.

Recently I found in my files the following quote in the cover article of the *New York Times Review of Books* for February 19, 1995, a review of "An Anthropologist on Mars" by Oliver Sachs: "When we open our eyes each morning, it is upon a world we have spent a lifetime *learning* to see (italics in original)," Dr. Sachs points out. "We are not given the world; we make our world

---

[17] Source: typescript of tape of presentation at SDSU, March 20, 1968.

through incessant experience, categorization, memory, reconnection. But when Virgil (the patient Dr. Sachs is discussing) opened his eye, after being blind for 45 years. . .there were no visual memories to support a perception. . .He saw, but what he saw had no coherence." Clearly Oliver Sachs, author of *Awakenings* and *The Man Who Mistook His Wife for a Hat* (among other books), conceptualizes his world in a fashion strikingly similar to James' "blooming, buzzing confusion" metaphor.

Language and Reality

For more than a decade between the early 1940s and the mid 1950s, I was deeply involved in the study of linguistics and semantics. I read widely, was active in professional organizations, and gave frequent talks on the subject. I had been particularly impressed by the writings of Benjamin Lee Whorf. Whorf, who died in 1941 at the age of 44, was by profession a fire prevention engineer and investigator for a Hartford, Connecticut, fire insurance company and by hobby an amateur linguist and anthropologist whose papers were presented before learned societies and published in top professional journals. Even some fifty plus years after his death, the bold hypotheses of this unusual amateur were still stimulating and controversial in professional circles. Like the ideas of William James and Robert Lynch, some of Whorf's ideas too began to take on renewed significance because they also seemed to lend credence to Alurista's views.

In the course of his investigations into linguistic relativity, Whorf had noted that certain deep differences in language structure between language groups often seemed to imply culturally differing ways of perceiving reality. The so-called Whorfian hypothesis (his hypothesis that the structure of one's language directly affects one's thought processes and behaviors) is based on the assumption that the picture of the universe differs from tongue to tongue, that each culture provides its members with its own peculiar ready-made way of viewing reality, and that language is the primary vehicle by which each culture's world view is transmitted and maintained. The next two paragraphs summarize one of Whorf's best known examples.

Hopi Plurals

In his study of the Hopi language, Whorf noticed that certain things that are plural in Standard Average European (SAE) languages are singular in Hopi. SAE languages, it turned out, apply plurality in two ways: to real plurals, that is objects such as ten trees or ten men or ten horses that can actually be seen together in one place at the same time ("perceptible spatial aggregates" in Whorf's terminology) and imaginary plurals, that is cyclical events such as ten days or ten steps forward or ten strokes on a bell ("metaphorical aggregates"). The Hopi apply plurality to real plurals only; to them, Whorf believed, this might mean that ten days or ten strokes are seen, not as plurals (different things), but as the same event reoccurring again and again.

Whorf thought that any cultural difference in how reality is perceived that is as great as this is likely to show up as a difference in behavior and he suggested that the Hopi practice of spending several days in ceremonial rituals in preparation for events such as planting crops might be a case in point. What we who speak and think in SAE languages unquestioningly perceive as several different days, the Hopi may, equally unquestioningly, be perceiving as the same day reappearing again and again. Just as it makes sense to us that one can prepare for and thus influence the later visits by the same person by what happens during the visit he is making now, so preparations on successive days may make similar sense to the Hopi.

The difference between the SAE plural and the Hopi plural is only one among several differences that Whorf points out. One of the most striking of these differences is the Hopi concept of time.[18] Unlike SAE languages which treat time as steadily flowing by in linear units that can be measured, the Hopi appear to treat the same phenomena as forming two vast nonlinear realms: one, the "Objective" (Whorf's SAE term, not the Hopi's)—that which already has happened or is happening now; the other, the "Subjective"—that which might happen but hasn't happened yet. Whorf claims that even without the concept of time as flowing-by-in-

---

[18] Described by Whorf in "An American Indian Model of the Universe," *Language, Thought, and Reality: Selected Writing of Bejamin Lee Whorf,* John Wiley & Sons, Cambridge and New York, 1956, pp. 57-64.

measurable-units, "the Hopi language is capable of accounting for and describing correctly, in a pragmatic or operational sense, all observable phenomena of the universe" [19]

All this provided one more of the reasons why I eventually found myself taking seriously Alurista's assertions about "irreconcilable contradictions" and "mutually exclusive ways of looking at reality." Whether Whorf was right or wrong in his conjecture about the Hopi ceremonial rituals, the evidence from his observations and the observations of other comparative linguists does suggest that the Hopi do live by a quite different view of reality than white western Europeans do. Certainly language structures are based upon and do have imbedded into them primitive understandings of physics representing differing early notions about reality. The structure of our SAE languages is based on its own assumptions about reality, some of which are incompatible with reality as modern physics understands it. Perhaps the most striking example of this dissonance is known as Zeno's paradox.

Zeno's paradox has been stated in a variety of ways; one of the briefest forms goes as follows: "If the tortoise has the start on Achilles, Achilles can never come up with the tortoise; for, while Achilles traverses the distance from his starting point to the starting point of the tortoise, the tortoise advances a certain distance, and while Achilles traverses this distance, the tortoise makes a further advance, and so on ad infinitum. Consequently, Achilles may run ad infinitum without overtaking the tortoise."[20]

The logic of Zeno's paradox is impeccable. It proves its point beyond possible argument. The trouble is, it is totally disproved by everyone's daily experience of reality. In fact, the paradox is a paradox only because it is an artifact of the language whose structure all members of our culture have agreed to accept. It is a remarkable demonstration of the fact that the structure of the grammar of SAE languages is based upon, and has embedded into it so deeply as to have become almost invisible, a very primitive notion of physics that simply doesn't fit reality—in this case, the reality of motion.

---

[19] Ibid, p. 58.
[20] *Encyclopedia Britannica*, 1970 Edition, Volume 23, p. 359

Mathematicians have long known this and have regularly had to create new "languages" based on more adequate assumptions. The calculus is one example; it is a language that was created specifically to account for the very defect that Zeno's paradox exposes. It does so by simply throwing away what one writer has called the tiny little "ghost of departed particles" of distance (derivative of "x") that the logic of our grammatical structure insists must remain! Motion is not the only concept that our language structure is ill equipped to handle; time is perhaps even more intractable. (Have you tried lately thinking about what came before the "beginning?". . .or just what will be left after the "end?" Try it sometime—it gives new meaning to the expression "blowing your mind!")

The question arises: are there other subtler assumptions that we believe and live by that are equally erroneous but are not so readily contradicted by daily experience? Notice how unconcernedly we have managed to accept our SAE concepts of motion and of time, difficulties and all. How many of us would ever have noticed any problem with talking about motion (a few mathematicians and other scholars possibly excepted) if Zeno of Elea hadn't pointed it out some 2,300 years ago?

Paranoia in a Soviet Airport

Not all defective conclusions, of course, result from assumptions embedded into our language structure. Many are idiosyncratic. For example, mention of Zeno's paradox brings to my mind a much later experience of my own that occurred in the Moscow airport on the first night of a 9,000 mile group tour of the Soviet Union just prior to the 1980 Olympic games in Moscow. I quote directly from a lengthy letter I sent to family and friends upon my return:

"Whenever our tour group arrived at a new airport, our *Intourist* guides immediately led us to a comfortable private waiting room off by ourselves. The first time this happened, my reaction was instant: just as I had anticipated, they (the Soviets) were making certain that we were not going to see anything we were not supposed to see. For half an hour or more, I moved restlessly around our waiting room, looking at items in locked souvenir counters, occasionally wandering to the doorway, standing there with one or two others looking out into the main part of the airport. Eventually two or three of the bolder members of our group ventured a short distance away from the doorway. Nothing happened. I joined them and we ventured further. Nothing happened. Soon we were roaming freely throughout the airport, watching native Russians on benches with their bundles waiting for their planes, and spending our kopecks for ice cream or souvenirs. The purpose of the private room, it turned out, was not to keep us in. It was to give us a secure place to leave our coats and hand luggage, a quiet place to rest or read. I learned something not very flattering about myself as I realized that nothing but my own paranoia had kept me restricted to that first waiting room for that first half hour that first night in a Soviet airport."

That experience still stands out in my mind as a prime example of how we live and behave in terms of the mental maps of reality that we have made instead of reality itself, this in spite of how easily our map can turn out to be in error. (Remember that silly line from the old-time vaudeville comedian's routine: "Are you going to believe me or your own lying eyes?")

I am aware that my soviet-airport "map," defective because of assumptions based upon inaccurate prior verbal information rather than direct experience of reality, is a very superficial thing compared to the Zeno's-paradox map which was defective because of assumptions deeply embedded into the very structure of the SAE languages themselves. My defective airport map quickly changed upon receipt of information based on direct experience— SAE languages remain unchanged despite information Zeno called to our attention some 2,300 years ago! Yet at the same time I am aware of how powerful a determiner of behavior my airport map was—had it not been for others in my group operating from less rigid maps, I might have remained confined by my map-imposed inaccurate information indefinitely.

Even though, as claimed, language does codify and preserve the unique characteristics that make different cultures truly different, even though it may in fact be the primary carrier of cultural differences, it is not the creator of them. Languages themselves are culturally determined, not biologically determined and can be lost in a matter of a generation or so. If Alurista was to be deemed correct, and I was becoming convinced that possibly he was, something else, something even more fundamental than language, must be at work. Otherwise, contrary to Alurista's assertion, any Chicano who has lost her/his primary language would be melting into the melting pot just as readily as anyone else.

The sum of all this is that I found myself becoming convinced that it was possible that differing basic core assumptions about the nature of reality could exist and also that perhaps they could survive and persist and influence behavior in ways that I had not previously realized. Though I could not (and still cannot) explain how this might occur, it seemed clear that something beyond language, possibly something operating at some subliminal level, must be the vehicle for their preservation and persistence. Perhaps it is through our very earliest preverbal impressions that we form our views of the nature of the reality about us, views some traces of which in some way somehow manage to persist.

But even after I had become convinced that it could happen, another question still remained. Is there any evidence anywhere that it actually does happen?

So in the next chapter my quest continues. . .

Chapter Ten

Cultural Differences Revisited

"The old men say so. . .They almost always know."
—Margaret Craven, *I Heard the Owl Call My Name*

To resume where I left off at the end of the previous chapter, not only had I found myself ready to accept the possibility that different cultures might be based on different assumptions about reality, but the whole idea had become increasingly intriguing to me. At the same time I remained reluctant to embrace it wholeheartedly. I was resistant to it for a number of reasons. I was resistant because to accept it was to challenge what I had previously assumed to be the natural order of things and hence, obviously, the one and only "truth." I was resistant because I did not like to acknowledge racial or ethnic differences; I preferred to think of all peoples as inherently "just people"—all alike under the skin. I was resistant because, like many of my fellow liberal whites, I felt that to acknowledge racial or cultural differences of any sort would somehow be giving aid and comfort to the Jensens and the Shockleys and others whose ideas I considered to be racist. It was as if by acknowledging that people of color could be different, I would be acknowledging that they could be considered inferior.

Nevertheless I continued to watch for evidence either to support or to refute the idea. Are there peoples who live, in part at least, by assumptions about reality that are fundamentally different from those held by my own white Euro-western patriarchal

117

(Anglo) world? If so, do traces of this persist even after their apparent assimilation into the Anglo world? Prospects for finding clear answers did not seem encouraging. The concept itself had an amorphous, cotton-candy-like lack of substance about it and, as I have pointed out earlier, all conceivable sources of hard comparative data were hopelessly contaminated. I had no idea where to look to find evidence.

As it turned out, the evidence found me. It turned up in my classrooms, it turned up in my consulting, it turned up in my reading. None of it was hard data. It came in the form of hints between the lines and glimpses behind the scenes. It came at a time when my awareness was being continually sharpened by my experiences inside CBB. Now, with my increasing sensitivity, when I began specifically looking for differences that implied different assumptions about reality, I found that I was seeing things in a light that I would not have seen them before. The accumulation of this soft evidence overcame any remaining reluctance. Even though this sort of evidence did not constitute rigorous proof, I became more and more convinced that there was something significant there. In the pages that follow, I will share some of the hints and glimpses whose cumulative impact led me to view the matter the way I do today.

Maria Elena's Grandmother

After Alurista's visits, I began to discuss in CBB and my other classes the possibility that there might be cultural differences in ways of relating to reality that persist, often undetected, and I began to express my interest in looking for evidence to either support or refute the idea. One of the very first times that I brought the topic up, one of my students, Maria Elena Garcia, spoke up and said that she thought she knew an example of the very thing that I was talking about. Her grandmother, Maria Elena told us, was very old. Recently a professor from one of the universities in the Los Angeles area had come to her home to interview her as part of an oral history project to record the memories of the older generation before they were lost forever. Despite her years, Mrs. Garcia was very alert and articulate, and the interview went along smoothly until the very end when the interviewer said to her, "Just one more question, Mrs. Garcia. If you had your life to live

over again, what things would you do differently?" Maria Elena
told us that for a moment her grandmother sat there looking
puzzled and then said, "But that is my life. . .That is my life. . .I
just told you my life."

In all the years since, I have yet to come across a more
striking example of two culturally different ways of relating to
reality interacting with each other than in this brief breakdown in
communication between the young Anglo university professor
and Maria Elena's Mexican-American grandmother. Yet I probably would not have recognized it as such if it had not been for
CBB and Alurista's challenge.

On a number of occasions over the years, Chicano students
in CBB have called my attention to the so-called "magical realism" in the writings of Latin-American authors, particularly Gabriel
Garcia Marquez, telling me that it captures for them in a very
special way the "feel" of traditional Mexican view of reality. I was
impressed by Garcia Marquez' novel *One Hundred Years of Soli-
tude* when I read it, but for me his "magical realism" did not seem
all that special, little more than an interesting blending of realism
with fantasy. The claims that others have made for it elude me,
and no one has been able to explain it in a way that I can grasp.
I wonder, though, if I may not be, like Maria Elena's grandmother,
missing the point because I am dealing with a cultural difference
which I do not comprehend.

African-American Brothers

On several occasions George Cox and I discussed the whole
topic of indigenous reality and its persistence. I had previously
told George that during the weekend in his home in Nashville I
had noted the automatic bonding between him and the two young
African-Americans from the Berkeley area. Although George did
not think of it in terms of different realities, he had been as aware
of the bonding as I had. Indeed, he reminded me about another
incident he and I had shared that he considered to be an even
better example of the same thing. It had occurred during our
second visit together to Rocky Boy. George and I were eating
breakfast together in the Four B's restaurant in Havre, Montana,
when two tall young African-American males entered the dining
area. Almost instantly they saw George and he saw them and he

rose from the table to meet and greet them half way. I remembered the incident. They had been basketball players from the local community college.

George pointed out that even despite the importance of our friendship, there was something that he shared with African-American strangers that he and I would never share. It made no difference that he had never seen those Havre basketball players before and that he probably would never see them again, he still felt some special bond almost like an electric current flash across the room. He said that this was not solely a male-bonding thing; it happened with "sisters" as well as "brothers" despite the often open antagonisms between the genders. He said he thought of this as something like family—you might not even like some of your family members but you had a special bond with them that no outsider could ever quite share. George was intrigued by my views about cultural differences in reality, but never fully convinced. He thought that whites probably have exactly the same reaction when they are in a predominantly Black country. I was not so sure that it would be the same.

Gittin Down

I also had similar conversations with Raymond Howard after he came to San Diego State. For twelve great years, until his health forced him to take a disability retirement, he and I were office mates, colleagues in CBB, and closest of friends. Raymond's background gave him an unusual perspective on this matter. He was from an African-American family that had lived in the state of Montana ever since the end of the Civil War, one of the small number of African-American families in the entire state. He spoke of what he called his "Black need to be with blacks," and of how important the occasional statewide picnics which were attended by almost every African-American family in the state had been to him when he was growing up. There were some things, he said, that he could be and feel only when in an all-black group. In his words, those picnics were the only times when he felt he could really "git down."

Raymond and I talked together a lot about what "gittin down" means. We both knew that, whatever it means, it was something he and I could talk about but never quite share, no matter how intimately we might share much of the rest of our lives. For Raymond, his black need to spend time exclusively with blacks was not something he had felt only while growing up in Montana; it was as much a need for him while he was living with his grandmother in Los Angeles or now in San Diego as it had been when living in Helena. This seems to me all the more noteworthy because I have never known any African-American more readily accepted by and better equipped to thrive in the white world than Raymond Howard. He and George Cox helped me to learn to live comfortably with the idea that there may well be some things in their reality that do not exist in mine.

Native American Indian Reality

As I look back now, I realize that those first years that I was back in San Diego (1972-1974) were particularly good years to be looking for evidence of basic core cultural differences. The era that we loosely refer to as "the sixties" was only then coming to a close. Interest in the indigenous Native American Indian way of life and world view was at a high level and many new materials were becoming available. The Native American Indian culture is the richest source I know of hints about and glimpses into the existence of an indigenous way of viewing the world that is quite different from that of the so-called "dominant" Anglo (Euro-western) society. Three books in particular that appeared in print between 1971 and 1973 stand out in my mind. They are *Touch the Earth*, (McLuhan, T. C., New York: Promontory Press, 1971); *Black Elk Speaks*, (New York: Simon & Schuster, 1972); and *I Heard the Owl Call My Name*, (New York: Doubleday & Company, 1973). In the summer of 1998, all three were still in print. The diaries of Anais Nin, an articulate believer that men and women differ markedly in the way they relate to reality (see next chapter) were also being published during these years.

Touch the Earth

This book is the one of the three that contributed the most to me at the time. Its subtitle, *A Self-Portrait of Indian Existence* describes it well. It contains a selection of almost 100 statements and writings by North American Indians plus more than fifty photographs that were taken in the early 1900s by the distinguished photographer, Edward S. Curtis, to record a people and a way of life that were about to vanish. It is the most accessible source that I know for reading in the Indians' own words their views of the wars and treaties and negotiations during the period of white western expansion—and their love for the way of life that had for so long been theirs. Among the voices included are such famous chiefs and warriors as Black Hawk, Sitting Bull, Crazy Horse, and Chief Joseph of the Nez Perces. In many of their statements these and other Indian leaders speak eloquently of their oneness with the earth and their environment, and their sense of unity and belongingness and the relatedness of all living things—in all an abundant source of evidence of how different their indigenous view of the world was from my own. (Small wonder the Native American Indian, like the Chicano, has found it so difficult to melt into the melting pot.)

I cannot resist sharing one of my favorite passages from *Touch the Earth*, even though it's content is only peripherally relevant to my purposes in this chapter. On June 14, 1744, the Indians of the Six Nations were invited by commissioners from Maryland and Virginia to send boys to William and Mary College; the next day the Indians declined as follows:

> *We know that you highly esteem the kind of learning taught in those Colleges, and that the Maintenance of our young Men, while with you, would be very expensive to you. We are convinced that you mean to do us Good by your Proposal; and we thank you heartily. But you, who are wise must know that different Nations have different conceptions of things and you will therefore not take it amiss if our ideas of this kind of Education happen not to be the same as yours. We have had some Experience of it. Several of our young People were formerly brought up at the Colleges of the Northern Provinces: they were instructed in all your Sciences; but, when they came back to us, they were bad Runners, ignorant of every means of living in the woods...neither fit for Hunters, Warriors, nor Counsellors, they were totally good for nothing.*
>
> *We are, however, not the less oblig'd by your kind offer, tho we decline accepting it; and, to show our grateful Sense of it, if the Gentlemen of Virginia will send us a Dozen of their Sons, we will take Care of their Education, instruct them in all we know, and make Men of them. (Touch the Earth, page 57)*

This is only one among many memorable statements in the book. Most, however, are more painful to read—filled with sorrow and nostalgia for the loss of the way of life and the land they had so dearly loved, and with sadness and bitterness about treacheries and treaties broken by the white man in taking it away from them.

I Heard the Owl Call My Name

It may seem strange to find a work of fiction included in the context of this particular chapter. However, there are many people, myself among them, who think that *I Heard the Owl Call My Name* is one of the most culturally sensitive novels ever written. It is the story of a young Anglican vicar assigned to an Indian village on the northwest coast of Canada so remote that it was accessible only by boat, and of his gentle introduction into a world dramatically different from his own. The elements of culture clash are dealt with in such a warm and sympathetic fashion that, fiction or not, the story is one of the most convincing presentations that I know. On almost every page, the young vicar is learning something new about the Indian community, and in the process something new about himself. As a reader, no doubt in part because of the many changes going on in my own life at the time, I was not only moved by the story, I found my personal understandings both enlarged and reinforced by it.

The following short excerpt gives some small hint of the nature of this book. It is part of a conversation between Mark, the young vicar, and his deckhand, Jim, a young native of the village recently returned home after working outside in a mill for a year. It is Mark's first day in the village and when he enters the vicarage, he discovers the small body of a drowned child inside. Mark asks Jim:

> "And why—why hasn't he been buried?"
> "Because no burial permit has been given. The chief councillor went at once to the nearest radio-telephone and summoned the RCMP (Royal Canadian Mounted Police), but no one has come yet."
> "Then we had better call again."
> "The constable will come today. The old men say so."
> "How do they know?"
> "How did they know you were coming today? They almost always know. Besides it is the first good day and he will come soon now. It is a five hour trip from Alert Bay, and he will want to get back before night, and he will be young, and he will be hard."
> "How do you know he will be young?"
> "An older man would not wait ten days." (*Owl*, pp. 24-25)

The old men somehow almost always know. The Anglo new-comer is looking for reasons. Jim, the young Indian, stands astride both cultures. This brief excerpt gives an example of the unusual cultural sensitivity with which the book portrays the coexistence of two very different worlds. *(I Heard the Owl Call My Name* was Margaret Craven's first novel, published when she was sixty-nine years old.)

Indians and Religion

Somewhere I have read that North American Indians had no word for religion before the white man came. They had no need for the concept—everything in their environment and their world of experience was spiritual. There were spirits in the rocks and in the plants, spirits in the lakes and in the hills. There were the spirits of their ancestors and the Great Spirit and the list goes on and on. I do not know whether my information that there was no word for religion was correct or not, but assume with me for a moment that it was. Think what the introduction of the strange new concept embodied by the word *religion* does. If, as the very existence of the new concept implies, certain things are religious, then the implication clearly also is that there are some things that are not. The two world views—one without a concept of religion and one with such a concept—become mutually exclusive. If, as claimed, Indians did not originally have such a concept, a part of their original way of viewing and living in the world died when it was introduced. What had been invisible and hence unquestioned was so no longer.

Eastern (Pan-Asian) Ways

I wish that I personally were more familiar with the whole realm of Eastern religions, wisdom, philosophies, etc. My limited experience is just enough to lead me to believe that it represents still another very different way of being in the world and of relating to reality. James Clavell caught some of this in his novel *Shogun* (New York: Dell. 1973) which also was published about this time. Even though his book is not entirely accurate either historically or culturally, his fictional story of a western seafarer's adventures ashore in early times in Japan conveys the notion of a clash of cultures extremely well. But what I find far more intriguing than anything in *Shogun* is the world view portrayed in Japanese samurai movies, especially the character of the blind samurai and the concept of "Ki."

For me, the concept of Ki (from Akido) is particularly fascinating. Apparently it is a concept that is impossible for my western mind to grasp because I don't really have words to describe it. It seems to have something to do with total awareness of one's environment and supposedly requires a state of extraordinary inner calm. It doesn't have to be visual—in fact it really isn't visual; it seems to transcend the five senses as I know them. There is a story of the Samurai Master who balanced a pillow above his door and then called his three sons, one at a time, to come to him. As the first son comes through the doorway, the pillow falls and hits him; the son whips out his sword and shreds the falling pillow to bits before it can reach the floor. To him, the Master says, "Go back to your quarters and practice, my son." As the second son comes through the doorway, he whips out his sword and shreds the falling pillow before it can even touch him. To him, the Master says, "Go back to your quarters and practice, my son." The third son refuses to come through the doorway. To him, the Master says, "You are a swordsman, my son."

I can remember when we Anglos didn't think much of acupuncture, either. Hmmmm.

I owe much to Alurista. My debt goes well beyond his assertions about a basic indigenous core and consequent irreconcilable contradictions. Thanks to the questions that his ideas raised in my mind, I shed my more naive view of culture and the role it plays in our lives and came to realize that the truly crucial, distinguishing characteristics of a culture are its shared ways of viewing and relating to reality, its shared assumptions that become accepted without question as the "natural order of things." What Alurista had started in me became nothing less than a total paradigm shift in the way I looked at culture and reality and cultural differences, a *sine qua non* of my re-educating.

As I look back over this chapter and the one preceding it, it is interesting to note to how great an extent the data upon which my shift was based were already available to me long before I met Alurista. It is a shift that might never have occurred, or at least not so rapidly, without the fortuitous combination of my exposure to CBB and to Alurista's challenge at very much the same time. I no longer have any clear idea of just how long it did take for it to take place. I do remember that in April of 1974—twenty months after my return to SDSU, forty months after I began to work with people of color—I for the first time went public in front of an audience of strangers with some of my newly evolving notions and questions about culture and reality and cultural differences; prior to this I had discussed these ideas only with my students and with a few of my closest colleagues and friends. Here is the story.

A Workshop in South Texas

I had been invited to conduct a workshop in south Texas for a group of graduate students and faculty from Pan American University in Edinburgh, Texas. The group consisted of 15-20 graduate students and faculty members, all but two or three of whom were Mexican-American. I no longer can remember what topic or topics the workshop was designed to cover; I do remember the final wrap-up session. One of the workshop participants had been with me and Dusty Wilson in the hotel room in Austin the night described earlier. One or the other of us made mention of that experience, and one thing led to another, and I answered a number of questions, and the group seemed interested, so finally I cast all my remaining reluctance aside and simply shared with them exactly where my thinking seemed to be taking me. It was a risk I ordinarily would not have taken. I had been burned early and often prior to this for presuming that I, a white male, had anything to tell people of color about being people of color.

I do not remember precisely what I said or didn't say at that final session nor how I said it. I spoke without notes so I have no way of knowing now to what extent my present ideas had evolved by that date. I am sure I mentioned Alurista and some of the other things I've mentioned in this chapter and possibly some from the chapter before it. I do remember that I was pleased and encouraged by the response that I received. I had said to them that this was the way things were beginning to seem to me based on my experiences and I had asked if any of my ideas spoke to their experiences as well. There was little or no disagreement with my hunches and there was much reinforcement for me since in so many ways my views seemed consistent with their own. This experience gave me the assurance that I needed and I have never turned back.

There was one comment, however, that particularly challenged me. It came at the very end of the final session when the one Anglo woman in the group said that she felt sad because, in her words, "We Anglo's don't have any culture of our own." There was no opportunity to deal with her comment at the time, but her words stayed with me. For some time thereafter I kept wondering about things that I might have said to her. And at the same time I began to realize that, despite my increasing conviction that cultures have basic underlying distinguishing characteristics that differentiate them from each other, I had been blithely going along without making much systematic effort to identify basic characteristics peculiar to my own.

That will be the next chapter.

Chapter Eleven

A Look at Anglo Male Reality

O wad some Pow'r the giftie gie us
To see oursels as others see us!
It wad frae mony a blunder free us,
And foolish notion. . .
—Robert Burns, "To A Louse"

The anecdote at the end of the previous chapter about the Anglo woman at the south Texas workshop who believed that "we Anglos don't have any culture of our own" illustrates a notion that I have found to be fairly common among Anglos. Her world of whiteness was so familiar to her that she wasn't consciously aware that she had any culture at all. As Anglos, we live for the most part in a monochromatic world. As long as we remain within it, many of the most powerful "white" assumptions by which our lives are governed remain unrecognized, and hence unquestioned. The white Navy officer I mentioned in chapter seven who "never thinks of himself as white" is another example. The Texas woman and that Navy officer are far from being alone in this respect, as the following will show.

Workshop in Cancun

Several years ago I conducted a workshop for couples in Cancun, Mexico. Each couple consisted of an American woman married to a Mexican national living and working in Mexico. Each of the white American women spoke of how the rich culture of her husband's Mexican heritage had filled a void she had felt as a white with no particular culture of her own. The women spoke in these terms at the very same time that they were participating in a workshop that they had organized precisely because they were finding it difficult to adjust in their marriages to certain aspects of their husbands' culture, because those aspects differed so greatly from their own.

"I don't know who it was that first discovered water but I am sure it wasn't a fish." This favorite aphorism of mine became almost a mantra during the four-day workshop. The American women and their Mexican husbands had first to identify the white cultural expectations that were being violated before they could begin to explore ways for reducing the stresses that these violations were causing. By the end of the workshop, the American women were no longer claiming that whites had no culture of their own.

The fish/water aphorism captures the essence of the paradigm shift that I mentioned in the preceding chapter, my coming to believe that the truly crucial, distinguishing characteristics of a culture are its shared ways of relating to and assumptions about reality. These assumptions are often so subtle and so all-pervasive that they become, like water to a fish, virtually invisible, as unobtrusive as the air we breathe. Invisible assumptions of this sort are not likely to get challenged or changed as long as we are largely unaware that they even exist. They operate subliminally. They are accepted without question as the natural order of things. They form the permanent foundations upon which cultures are built. Awareness of the nature of these invisible assumptions is essential for understanding differences between cultures. My purpose in this chapter is to report what my musings have led me to believe is one of the characteristics, perhaps *the* one characteristic, of my white Euro-western patriarchal (Anglo) cultural view of reality that most clearly distinguishes us from others.

Seeing the Invisible

How does one go about seeing the invisible? I have no magic mirror. Yet if our invisible assumptions are ever to become subject to examination and possibly changed, we need to make them become as visible to us as we possibly can. I know of only one way to make this happen. Like the fish that needs to be away from water in order to discover it, like the white Navy officer who needed to see a black face in order to become aware of how aware he was of his own whiteness, we Anglos need what I call a "mirror of non-whiteness" in order for our invisible white assumptions to become visible to us. I don't know who it was who first discovered water but I am sure it wasn't a fish.

Incidentally, for people of color, life is very different from the typically monochromatic life of the Anglo. Rarely if ever do people of color find themselves in a world into which the Anglo culture has not encroached. I am inclined to believe that there may be a lot of truth in the claim I hear from time to time from people of color that they understand Anglos better than we Anglos understand ourselves.

Cultural Plunge as Mirror

The term "cultural plunge" is not only an apt description of the last twenty years of my professional life, it is also the term I used for the activity that I most strongly recommended to the students in the "Social and Cultural Determinants of Behavior" course that I taught for many years for students not enrolled in the CBB. I defined "cultural plunge" as "to do something that violates (gets one away from) one's own culture, and to observe and record how you feel and what you learn." I stressed that the primary purpose was not to learn about other people and other lifestyles, important as that may be—it was "not to be like a field trip to observe animals in a zoo." The purpose of the plunge was to provide a mirror in which each student might catch a glimpse of her/his own unexamined assumptions.

Of course, the invisible unexamined assumptions underlying our white culture are not really invisible—very much the opposite. Like water to a fish, they are so all-pervasive and so obvious that they simply go unnoticed. They are likely to remain unnoticed—and their importance unexamined—unless something such as seeing ourselves in a mirror of non-whiteness brings them to our attention. My experiences with persons from other cultures (especially my nineteen years in CBB) have been one continuing cultural plunge and the mirror that has helped me to get a glimpse into my own unexamined Anglo male assumptions.

Certain types of situations have proven especially likely to produce new insights (or, more often, reinforce old ones) for me.

They are situations in which I (1) find that I am feeling uncomfortable and am not quite sure why, (2) am surprised or blindsided by a reaction to something I have said or done, (3) sense that I have unintentionally put my foot in my mouth, and (4) get a negative reaction from a person of color that I consider to be undeserved or unfair. There were times, I confess, when I failed to get the point until friends like Maria Nieto Senour or George Cox or Raymond Howard pointed it out to me. Sometimes what I have learned has been strictly idiosyncratic but often I have discovered traces of my cultural heritage that have been persisting unnoticed.

The cumulative evidence which I have obtained, partly through experiences of my own in CBB, partly through what I have experienced vicariously by observing Anglo students in their interactions with non-whites, and partly by my various readings, has led me to conclude that to a remarkably large extent the most significant things about what it means to be Anglo can be traced back to a single powerful seminal difference. At first glance, this difference may seem so simple and so obvious that it can't possibly be that important. Initially I did not sense its implications myself. In the next paragraphs I present this one most critical difference for your consideration and try to explain why I find it so important.

A Separated Reality

The characteristic that I now believe most clearly and consistently differentiates the Anglo (white Euro-western patriarchal) world view from that of other cultures, especially those closer to their indigenous roots, seems to me to be the extent to which the Anglo world view is based on a more "separated" view of reality. In the Anglo view of reality, individuals see themselves as more distinct and separate, both from other persons and from their environment. Anglos do not have as much feeling of oneness, of connectedness with others and with the rest of the earth, as do those whose cultures are closer to their indigenous roots. To be Anglo means to live with a much greater sense of separateness in your relationship to your external reality.

For example, it seems to me that Maria Elena's grandmother couldn't handle the interviewer's final question (page 118) because there was no way she could separate herself and her life from its actual reality, not even hypothetically. To the young Anglo professor, it was a perfectly reasonable question. In both of Alurista's examples, the individualistic-versus-collectivistic and the competitive-versus-cooperative, the Anglo is characterized by separateness from other people and the Chicano by connectedness with other people. The entire thrust of Native American religion and spirituality is on oneness with the whole earth, on unity and wholeness and a sense of belonging. George Cox and his fellow African-Americans in the restaurant in Montana and that weekend in his home in Tennessee had some instant, special bond of interconnectedness that I couldn't quite understand nor be part of but could only accept as fact.

The African-American usage of the term *brother* for all black males and *sister* for all black females (and perhaps *soul* as well) may not be pure happenstance. Even the Eastern martial arts concept of *ki* implies a special kind of interconnectedness between person and world, a kind of interconnectedness so totally incomprehensible to my detached Anglo mind that my almost irresistible reaction is to deny the possibility of its existence.

An Anglo Overlay

Before I go on to elaborate on the far-reaching implications of this greater separateness of the white Euro-western patriarchal (Anglo) way of viewing the world, I want to make it clear that while I consider this to be a fundamental Anglo characteristic, I am fully aware that it is by no means limited to Anglos. Far from it. In this modern complex world, virtually all persons living today, regardless of color or gender or where they may be on this shrinking globe, have come to adopt some aspects of the dominant Anglo separated world view to some degree or other. Not only Alurista's Chicanos but also African-Americans and Native American Indians and all of the other "visible ethnics" (including Margaret Mead's little native kids on their remote south sea islands) are actually *mestizos*, that is, culturally and psychologically a mixture.

Superimposed on all non-white non-Euro-western peoples today, there is always to some degree what I refer to, admittedly imprecisely, as an "overlay" of Anglo reality. Sometimes this internal duality of indigenous and Anglo realities is obvious. It was painfully apparent at the panel of the six Native American Indian women at D-QU; all six were visibly in conflict inside, caught between conflicting allegiances to the values of two clearly incompatible world views, although they were divided three and three as to which should prevail. The "two-ness" of the African-American of which W. E. B. DuBois writes (which I mentioned in the same context) is another vivid example. So is Raymond's need to "git down." More often the internal conflict is deeply hidden. Underneath the Anglo overlay, there may somehow continue to persist some traces, however faint, of a virtually invisible core of indigenous reality (as Alurista claimed) somehow surviving despite every effort on the part of the Anglo culture to eradicate it.

Indigenous Cores

By "hidden, invisible indigenous cores" (the sort of thing Alurista was talking about), I do not mean obvious, conscious things like speaking French instead of German, or believing in Catholicism instead of Protestantism or Buddhism or Voodooism. As important and as powerful as language and religion are, they are conscious, clearly visible behaviors and they can be lost in one generation. I have come to believe that there are also things that can't be lost, or at least don't get wiped out in one generation, and that these things must represent something even more fundamental than language and religion. My guess is that they are traces of some basic world view passed down by the culture that still at some level dictate what one thinks reality is—not something that has been learned in any conscious way and can be readily unlearned later, but something that is simply absorbed somehow at some time and forever thereafter simply assumed. Remember Whorf's Hopi plurals. Remember Zeno's paradox. There are things one simply knows and can't explain—things one never feels any need to think about or to explain.

I am not at all sure how, or even if these indigenous cores survive, although what little evidence I have been able to gather leads me to think that they do. Anglo culture is very efficient at eliminating and supplanting large parts of entire cultures—all the parts that it has names and/or explanations for, all the parts it understands. It may be that, as one of my colleagues used to insist, when the Anglo culture can't put a name on or explain something, it either considers it unimportant or denies that it exists! Perhaps the core is made up mostly of nonverbal, nonlinear, non-intellective (meaning unexplained) stuff; perhaps it is stuff learned through body language, tactile experience, or modeling behaviors; perhaps it is preverbal stuff. Someone has said that "culture is hearth-based" and certainly we are all warmed by the hearthside long before we are formed by the language we will one day learn to use. Maybe this core is passed along verbally in disguise through stories, myths, songs, dreams, games, things learned subliminally. I don't know. I doubt if it can be known. I suspect that if it could be and ever were to be known, the Anglo culture could—and probably would—soon find a way to wipe it out!

The differences which remain may be subtle and elusive, but they may be extremely important. My hunch is that there are many people who are trying to make themselves fit into a world view that is not their own—understandably so because that is where so many of the payoffs in this world are. (More about that later.) The tragic result is, many of them feel inadequate and that something must be wrong within themselves, because deep inside they sense that somehow things just don't fit together quite right. Actually, it seems to me very possible that nothing is wrong within them—that surviving traces of the interconnectedness of their original cultural inheritance don't permit them to fit totally into the separateness of Anglo reality without feeling torn apart inside.

Women's Reality

Moreover, my hunch is that what is true for people of color—that members of all groups have an increasingly heavy overlay of Anglo reality superimposed over their own way of relating to reality—is equally true for women; that is, if you are a woman, you too are probably being bent out of shape by being forced into the mold imposed upon you by the harsh veneer of the dominant patriarchal Anglo society, and that it is not natural—or healthy—for you, either. It is not as easy for women to deny their own interconnectedness to Mother Earth as it is for men. Women are inescapably more intimately aware than most men of their own biorhythms, of their relationship to the lunar month, of their role in the sequence of the creation of life, and consequently of their interconnectedness with other persons and with the world around them. Underneath the patriarchal "separated" overlay that covers us all, women, like people of color, probably retain some still surviving inner core of greater interconnectedness.

My view here has been expressed well by the author and diarist, Anais Nin, who years ago maintained that men and women relate to reality very differently. She wrote that it was the special role of the woman artist to supply the critical link between—using her terms—the "earth elements" (women's reality) and "man's fatal detachment" (male reality). Nin was one of the famous group of expatriate American artists living in Paris following World War I. Her diaries were immensely popular when first published during the 1960s and 1970s, but less so later, partly I suspect because she was not interested in the economics side of women's struggles and hence not in line with mainstream interests of the feminist movement. I have recently seen large displays of her works in bookstores, which suggests that a resurgence of interest in her work may be taking place.[21]

The Brave New World of Cyberspace

As I write this chapter, I wonder about the discomfort that I, an aging male, am currently experiencing in the brave new world of cyberspace. I seriously wonder if the discomfort I experience in the strangeness of a digitalized electronic world with ground rules so different from anything in my own reality may not at some level be analogous to the discomfort experienced by persons with strong indigenous interconnectedness roots—or by women, too, for that matter—when trying to accommodate to the separateness of white Euro-western patriarchal reality. It's difficult to be smart in a world with ground rules different from one's own. It is particularly difficult since so often the differences remain invisible to all parties involved.

There may be a serious truth behind the recently popular humor about adults calling upon their six-year-olds to show them how to program the VCR or operate the computer. I am a neophyte in the world of computers. I am personally discovering that

---

[21] Nin, Anais, *Diaries*. New York: Harcourt, Brace & World, Vol. 1 (1966), Vol. 2 (1967), Vol. 3 (1969), Vol. 4 (1971), Vol. 5 (1974).

I am stupid indeed compared to young children I have watched as I begin to branch out from basic word processing into the realms of e-mail and the Internet. I find that I bring to this new arena a bunch of preconceived notions in the form of my linear assumptions about space and size and direction that I am trying to think with, and have trouble discarding even though on a cognitive level I know that such dimensions have little or no relevance in the strange new electronic world that I am trying to understand.

It is a humbling experience for me with my history of being a quick learner. I am once again the dumb intern floundering on someone else's turf. I can see that the turf is changing underneath my feet, but I still can't quite seem to adjust to the change. I try, but I just don't seem to get it. I learn, but I learn by rote. Nothing comes to me intuitively. (I wonder if what I tend to think of as intuitive may not often be an instance of tapping into some unrecognized inner core of early cultural learnings.) If I forget one step, I am reduced to blind trial and error, and I have learned that one error in cyberspace can be very unforgiving. One misstep and a block of print can disappear forever. So I find that I freeze from fear of the consequences of error and resist trial.

I am reminded of a story told by a college friend who was driving an ambulance with the Allied Forces fighting Rommel in North Africa early in World War II. On one occasion when his ambulance broke down he was left alone by the side of the road. He tried vainly to locate the trouble, shaking a few wires and tightening or loosening a few connections all to no avail. Then a passing vehicle called back for a mechanic to help him. Soon a little Aussie mechanic drove up, took one look under the hood and uttered these memorable words: "Who the fucking fuck fucked up this fucking fucker?" When it comes to computers, I find myself immobilized by my fear that I may become the guilty one who. . .

Harmony vs. Mastery

Why, some may be asking, do I make such a big deal about Anglos viewing self and world as more separate? I grant that on the surface it may seem both obvious and simple—but its implications turn out to be profound. The more I explore, the more amazed I become at how far-reaching the consequences of this particular difference in way of viewing reality turn out to be. First of all, it is a genuine difference, one observed over and over again, between Anglo reality and most others. Further, it is a difference that completely reverses the age-old relationship between humankind and nature. Throughout most of the history of the species, humankind has seen itself as puny and powerless in comparison to the awesome forces of nature; always before, humankind has striven to live in harmony with nature and has seen itself as only one among the many parts of the natural world. But, with the emergence of a more separated view of reality, the forces of nature have become "something-separate-out-there" to be predicted and controlled. In our world today, we expect to be able to predict and control and tend to be surprised whenever we aren't able to do so.

The key words are "harmony" and "mastery"—seeking to live in harmony with the forces of nature on the one hand versus seeking mastery (i.e., prediction and control) over them on the other. For several centuries, the trend has clearly been away from harmony and toward mastery—a change of enormous consequence indeed. As Alurista and so many others—Native American spokespersons, Nelson Mandela's mentor, etc.—have pointed out, in the world view of indigenous peoples, people belong to the land, to Mother Earth. In the separated Anglo view, the land belongs to people, property rights become more important than human rights, possessions more important than people, and the resources of the earth something to be exploited. Euro-western peoples did not invent this viewpoint—more likely, it evolved because of the results it produced—but clearly in today's times Anglos have come to epitomize it. And it is due to the results produced by the replacement of "harmony with" by "mastery over" that the white Euro-western society has gradually over the past four or five centuries been able to assume its current position of dominance.

Scientific Objectivity

The emergence of the Anglo separated world view with its focus on "mastery over" made possible the emergence of the age of scientific objectivity and technological progress. Scientific objectivity requires an observer who is separate from the object observed. This in turn divides the world into "in here" and "out there," into subject and object—subject meaning the detached observer and object the person or thing from which she/he is separate. For some perversely paradoxical reason, this seems to have led to a worship of objectivity and a prejudice against anything subjective. The scientific method denies the reality of all but the objective. Data must be replicable—otherwise they are rejected. In today's scientific world we live by the assumption that, as Theodore Roszak put it, there is but "one way of gaining access to reality. . .and this is to cultivate a state of consciousness cleansed of all subjective distortion, all personal involvement."[22] Roszak's book, while for the most part now sadly out of date, includes a chapter entitled "The Myth of Objective Consciousness," which still remains the best statement I know describing our technocratic, objective, Anglo world view.

The Anglo world dismisses any belief based on nonreplicable data by labeling such beliefs freaky, or primitive, or superstitious, or childish, or hallucinations. The church is granted an exemption, but only as long as it is speaking of another world. Any serious claims in this world for the validity of such subjective data as dreams, or omens, or auras, or premonitions, or the *I Ching*, etc., are dismissed in just those terms. Anything that cannot be explained does not exist. When we make the statement that "there must be some explanation!" we mean that there must be a logical, linear, objective explanation, or else it doesn't exist.

From this point of view, UFO's, ESP, psychokinesis, parapsychology, *Ki*, etc., (and, until recently, acupuncture as well) simply do not exist since they cannot be logically explained. The Anglo world view doesn't pay serious attention to anything subjective/intuitive or imaginary/fanciful—or anything that can't be verbally and logically explained. Note the scorn in expressions like, "you just made that up," or "it's just your imagination," or "another old wives' tale." This may help explain how, assuming that there is such a thing as a "hidden, indigenous inner core" as I have come to believe, traces of an indigenous reality may have survived despite the heavy Anglo overlay. Perhaps it survives because the Anglo world doesn't recognize that it actually exists.

[22] See Roszak, Theodore, *The Making of a Counter Culture*, New York: Doubleday & Company, Inc. 1969, p. 208.

The Good Things in Life

The emergence of a culture for which the norm is to view the world as something-out-there-to-be-mastered-and-controlled was a necessary precondition to, and is largely responsible for, the remarkable way that scientific progress and technology have flourished, and for the ever larger, ever more complex projects that are constantly being taken on. Without the emergence of this world view, we could not have had jet planes, antibiotics, polio vaccines, men-on-the-moon, the "information highway," modern health care, scientific agricultural production—the list goes on and on and on. Most of what today we so often refer to as "the good things in life" are dependent on modern scientific progress, which in turn is dependent upon scientific objectivity, which in turn requires the detached world view today epitomized by what we term the dominant society. It is the Anglo world's success in providing us with "the good things in life" that explains why the dominant society has become so dominant.

A "Cuppa Coffee"

The good things in life are not limited to the big things. Consider a cup of coffee. I did just that not so long ago. While driving north along Route 99 between Bakersfield and Fresno, I decided I would like a cup of coffee. I knew that a mini-mart or a coffee shop or some fast-food place was sure to show up within a mile or two. That thought launched me into a memorable fantasy. I began to try to think of all the people who would have had to have been involved in order for that cup of coffee to be waiting for me so conveniently that I could count on it being there just when and where I wanted it. I thought first of the South American pickers and growers and processors and then of those involved in the packaging and sales and transportation of the coffee to the U.S. Then I thought of the employees and employers and the owners and the builders and the financial backers of the shop at which I would get my coffee. Then I began to think of the numerous other long lists of people who must have been involved in providing the raw materials that went into the production of the car in which I was riding and the selling and delivery of it, and of the gasoline it was using, and then the people who built the highway on which I was driving and those who supplied and delivered the materials and the equipment that had been needed, and then the numerous taxpayers who had paid for it, etc., etc. That fantasy remains memorable for me because neither before nor since have I found myself so completely caught up in a euphoric awareness of, and appreciation for, my connectedness to the literally thousands and thousands and thousands of other people to whom I am indebted for the availability of trivial things which I ordinarily take for granted such as my anticipated "cuppa coffee."

Sure enough, at the very next exit from the freeway, there waiting for me was a coffee shop.

Dominance of the Anglo World View

Systems with the size and complexity of those in my "cuppa coffee" fantasy can only be produced by large organizations—big businesses and big governments. Bigness requires ever more efficient and complicated forms of organization. The management of organizations with departments made up of divisions and subdivisions, and an almost unlimited number of further levels of subsubdivisions, each with specialized functions, is only made possible by a hierarchy of authority and communication along these channels. Vital decisions are necessarily made by persons further and further separated from the persons and activities directly affected by them. It is no accident that a culture of separateness rather than one of togetherness assumed the lead in developing the organizations of bigness that we are so dependent upon today.

Indeed, the Anglo world view is so good at the things that it is good at that time and again it quickly dominates any other world view and typically eventually destroys it. It is so good, when it is good, that it is sometimes hard to consider any other alternative. It promises—and delivers—so many material benefits that it is understandable why it has increasingly become the dominant world view. It is so good that more and more it appears to be taking over; the overlay being plastered on so heavily is apparently quite capable of snuffing out all other world views. It is quite understandable why most Anglos and many people of color willingly fall into the trap of believing that it is superior. But it is a trap. Along with all its advantages, it has its drawbacks, its Achilles' heel.

The Flip Side

A closer look at the Anglo world's dependence on scientific objectivity and separateness reveals what a double edged sword it actually is. Objectivity and separateness do permit us to make greater use of, and control more of, our environment; they also permit us to plunder and destroy it. They permit us to kill off the buffalo, to wipe out endangered species, to strip mine and deforest the hills, to wash away the top soil, to upset and destroy the ecosystem. Sometimes the consequent destruction is unforeseen, unexpected, and unintended; sometimes it is the direct consequence of greed and simply not caring.

Objectivity and separateness do permit us to create the ever larger and more complex systems and subsystems (societies and organizations) that enable us to enjoy all those material things that make up what we call the "good life" (including my cup of coffee, the restaurant at which I got it, the car I was driving, and the highway I was driving on); in the process, the very size of these same organizations creates a climate of alienation that is damaging the quality of life at the same time that it is improving it. The larger and more complex and more efficient our organizations become, the more they lead to the depersonalization of the individual. People come to be seen merely as cogs in a machine, as interchangeable components. The welfare of the organization becomes more important than the welfare of any individual person, and the individual is left feeling alienated, disconnected, alone, a stranger in a world that promised so much.

Organizers and Improvisers

Once when I was on a vacation tour in South America, I struck up an acquaintance with a fellow tourist, a German businessman who had been a longtime resident of Peru. At one point after our tour bus had encountered a number of delays and it was apparent that we were not going to make a crucial connection, a number of us were becoming more and more concerned. My German traveler friend reassured us. "Don't worry," he said. "South Americans are the world's poorest organizers but the world's greatest improvisers." He was right. Everything worked out.

Ignore for a moment, if you will, the paternalistic tone and the stereotyping of the remark. I was struck at the time and still am by how aptly that statement captures the comparative strengths of two ways of being in the world—the separated Anglo way with its impersonal, complex, efficient organizations and the interconnected indigenous way with its personal, creative, spontaneous improvisations. The organizer is future oriented while the improviser functions primarily in the here-and-now. This suggests some deeply rooted cultural basis for the differences in cultural attitudes towards time that are so often poked fun at—the compulsive adherence to the constraints of external time in the future-oriented world on the one hand, and the primacy given to the internal mood-of-the-person-at-the-moment in the here-and-now world on the other. There is so much to be said for both. Too bad our Anglo world is so insistent that it be either/or.

The Zocalo at Noon

I once heard my colleague Maria Nieto Senour say, "When I am in Mexico and some friend says to me, 'I'll meet you at the Zocalo at noon tomorrow,' I know that that means that she may be there at noon, that she may arrive about two, that she may not come at all, and that if she does come she may well have her aunt and two cousins with her."

Maria said it fondly—most Anglos I know would be thinking, "What a lousy way to run a railroad!"

That sums it up in a nutshell.

But isn't it odd? Why is it that we Anglos speak of our Latino neighbors south of the border a bit patronizingly as the *mañana* people while we are the ones who are so preoccupied with clocks and schedules and planning for the future that we have almost lost our ability to live in and enjoy the existential moment?

Something to think about. . .

Chapter Twelve

The Anglo Stake in Cultural Pluralism

"The unleashed power of the atom has changed everything except our way of thinking, thus we drift toward catastrophe."
—Albert Einstein

During my lifetime there have probably been more changes in transportation, communication, information, health care, food production and who knows how many other areas than during the entire span of previous recorded history. One of the most important consequences of the Anglo way of relating to the world is the ever-accelerating rate of change that it is producing. The trouble is that change has been taking place just as rapidly on its negative flip side as it has on its positive side. Capacity for destruction grows as rapidly as capacity for production. The Anglo way is perfectly capable of eventually destroying all life on this planet.

Endangered Species

We may end up paying a terrible price for the presumed benefits our Anglo way of life is providing for us. The species we wipe out next may be our own. Consider for a moment a few of the possibilities: there could be some unpredictable "secondary consequence" (remember how the use of DDT on insects almost wiped out the California pelican); or some new laboratory-created immune resistant disease could be inadvertently (or deliberately) released into the general population; or there could be some unintended nuclear chain reaction or by-product of nuclear war such as nuclear winter; or there could be some catastrophe no one has even thought of yet. After all, only a few years ago no one except a few science fiction buffs had ever thought of the ones I've mentioned. The possibilities are many, any one of which would suffice. Whether such a catastrophe results from ignorance, accident, or mere irresponsibility is irrelevant; the result would be the same.

As you can see, I have a deeply pessimistic streak in me. I believe that unless it is somehow checked, our dominant Anglo culture may well be rushing us pell-mell, lemming-like, towards destruction. It has so much going for it that I think it is very unlikely that it will (or even can) be checked. The productive side is so inextricably enmeshed with the destructive side that the two cannot readily be separated. As the production conglomerates that we have created increasingly transcend international boundaries, we become more and more subject to the tyranny of the "bottom line." I don't see us likely to turn back the clock, to give up the advantages that size and complexity have brought, whatever the long-term cost. In fact, I can't even see me doing so—I remember how much I wanted that cuppa coffee! Never underestimate the power of NIMBY (not-in-my-backyard) as a barrier to intelligent social action. Indeed, for all I know, we may well be too late already; even if we do try, I am not at all certain that irreversible processes have not already been started.

One Last Metaphor

Our Anglo dominated society today is sitting on a social-cultural San Andreas fault. Earthquake-like tensions resulting from simultaneously coexisting opposing forces are steadily building up and eventually something is going to break loose. One source of tension: at the same time that technological advances are steadily accelerating the rate of social change, social systems are simultaneously becoming such complex interlocking interdependent networks that they are increasingly resistant to change. Note the frustrations involved in adopting the metric system or in reaching agreement on whether to drive on the left hand or the right hand side of the road.

Another tension: at the same time that our increasingly complex social order is steadily increasing its ability to put down resistance against the status quo with newly developed weapons and other technical devices such as secret surveillance techniques and control of the media, it is simultaneously becoming increasingly vulnerable to disruption by even a very small group of individuals. Note not only the development of attache-case-size bombs, but also the disruption that would result from a dozen strategically abandoned cars at the peak of urban rush hour traffic or a few well placed interruptions in the intricate networks required for the transmission of electricity. The Internet offers a potential for abuse on a scale that wouldn't have been possible without it. We are sitting on a social-cultural San Andreas fault and eventually something is likely to give. What's your guess? How long before the Great Quake? How long before we all will be striving to live within the security of gated compounds?

The implications of the above are serious. Someone, I believe it was the futurist Michael Marien, maintained years ago that the most severe problem facing the future of our emerging knowledge-based society is the growth of ignorance, which he defined as the gap between what we need to know and what we do know. He pointed out that our society had already long since moved beyond dependence upon experts to the point of choosing between disagreeing experts. What are the implications of this for a democratic society? We know from programmed instruction that if learning steps are too great, no learning takes place. By the same token, if the environment changes too rapidly, the learning steps needed for survival can become so great that no learning (adaptation, evolution, whatever) can take place and the species will perish. And you wonder why I am pessimistic?

The Anglo Stake

I am pessimistic but not a pessimist. If it is not already too late to reverse our pell-mell rush to self-destruction—and as I have just said, quite frankly I fear that it may be—I can see one faint glimmer of hope. If we are to have any chance to survive, I believe that our Anglo dominated world must recognize the importance of making room for more than one way of viewing reality and must realize that to continue exclusively along our present path is virtually certain eventually to destroy the human race. We must reexamine our arrogant Anglo male ethnocentrism and I only know of one mirror in which we can get a look at those otherwise invisible and unexamined assumptions of ours that are propelling us into trouble. That mirror is exposure to cultures holding views different from our own.

I see cultural pluralism as the "best hope" mirror for our survival. This means ending our cycle of racism and doing away with the melting pot, the everyone-melt-into-our-Anglo-pot-with-us idea. It means promoting a more pluralistic society by encouraging rather than discouraging ethnic identity movements and the women's movement, encouraging them not to abandon, but to get ever more deeply in touch with, their inner cores. It means that the impersonal, complex, efficient Anglo way of being in the world and the personal, creative, spontaneous indigenous way must learn to coexist as equal partners. Each has much to contribute to the other. (The emergence of the movement to encourage males to "get in touch with their feminine side" suggests possibilities.) It means identifying those things in the Anglo male world which can and must be changed and those which can and should be retained. It means identifying those aspects which are healthy and those which are toxic, and then taking active steps to eradicate the latter. It may mean giving up some of the good things in life that we enjoy today in return for a better future. Perhaps for any future at all!

All this may not be possible—the positive and the negative sides may not be separable. Or we may not have the will to make the effort—our Anglo track record for making short term sacrifices for long term gain has not been good. I wish the odds were better. Despite creating a world so complex, so impersonal, so out of control that it may well be destroying itself, my Anglo world has created some of the noblest dreams of all— "We hold these truths to be self-evident, that all men (and women) are created equal. . ." These are dreams worth saving. It will be the one last great irony if the world that dreamed these dreams is the world that planted the seeds of its own destruction. I wish the odds were better. Given my premises, and to me they do not seem at all unreasonable, I can only conclude that our *one slim hope for avoiding self-destruction* may well lie in obtaining input from a variety of world views by toning down our runaway eth-nocentrism and breaking the cycle of racism and promoting cultural pluralism. The odds are slim but the stakes are high. The Anglo stake in cultural pluralism may well be nothing less than the survival of the human race.

It was thirty-two years ago this year (year 2005) that George Cox and I led a group of whites and African-Americans from five southeastern states on a week-long cultural exchange to Rocky Boy's Reservation in Montana (page 28). It was thirty-two years ago this year that Rick LaPointe's cousin was killed at Wounded Knee. It was thirty-two years ago this year that I heard tribal elder Sam Windyboy, Sr.'s prayer that the Great Spirit help the white man to "see the error of his ways and stop his destruction of Mother Earth." Today my fondest wish for all that I love is that one day my Anglo world will hear and heed those words.

It's a whole new ball game, folks. Which side are you on?

WATER?

Reproduction of a large color drawing done some years ago by one of my students to illustrate my oft-repeated fish/water aphorism. See pages 63 and 130-131. DDM

Appendix A

More About CBB

This supplment is included in order to provide additional information about CBB for those interested in knowing more about the origins, nature and successes of the program that was such an important source of the ideas expressed in this book. It is a supplement to Part II (CBB, An Island of Diversity), which should be read first since, as much as possible, this does not duplicate it.

I. The Building of the Dream

It was in the fall of 1972 that I returned to San Diego State University. My path had led me back to the very place that two years before I had left in hopes of finding a setting in which to work with people in a way that was less hierarchical than the faculty-student relationship traditional in most universities. Two years had changed a lot of things. Now my dream of working in a more congenial setting included working with people of color. Now I realized that it was here where I was already known that I would have my best chance to translate my dream into reality.

I returned knowing that my dream would not be easy to articulate to others—it was still vague, even to myself—and it departed radically from traditional university ways. The academic year 1972-73 was to be a year of transition for me. It was a time for figuring out more specifically just what I wanted to do and how I wanted to do it, and for finding out if the university would let me do it. My feelings were mixed. It was with considerable trepidation as well as high anticipation that I resolved to push ahead and find out if I was dreaming a possible dream.

The Original Dream

My original idea, if not an impossible dream was certainly an immodest one. I sincerely believed that what I had in mind would both produce a better program for training counselors than any program I had ever developed before and at the same time provide me with an emotionally healthy space in which to work. I wanted to create a "learning community" in which faculty and students would relate with each other the way I had related with the folks with whom I had been working during my sabbatical leave—as equal partners (let me emphasize the word *equal*) working side by side on some important task. The task I had in mind was cross-cultural counseling.

Awareness of the importance of cross-cultural counseling was increasing in 1972 so my timing was right. And it had another important advantage—it offered precisely the kind of situation in which it was most reasonable to expect faculty and students each to bring different but essential expertise to a learning community. Faculty could bring an understanding of conventional counseling skills and theories; students, especially students from cultures with a less individualistic focus and more dependence upon family guidance and group sanctions, could bring direct-life-experience-based understandings of differing cultural ways and world views. The focus on cross-cultural counseling made the sort of learning climate that I wanted to create easier for my colleagues to understand and accept.

The idea, as it originally began to take form, was to bring together two or three faculty members and twenty to thirty students—hopefully many of them persons of color—to conduct a Community Counseling Center (or Help Center or Crisis Center) at some off-campus location somewhere in the inner city. San Diego State had a large graduate program in counselor education, at that time granting well over 100 master's degrees annually; the program I had in mind merely asked for a "piece of the action."

Our selection process would be designed to identify a group of students who together would represent as diverse a pool of resources as we could find. We would give more weight to the unique life experiences (family or cultural background, lifestyle, prior employment, volunteer work, etc.) that each student could bring to the group than we would to her/his test scores or prior grade point averages. Most important of all, this would provide our students with opportunity to work closely in cooperation with others culturally different from themselves while in the process of learning to become effective counselors for clients from cultures other than their own.

As I envisaged it, instead of typical formal courses with required textbooks and conventional assignments, we would utilize workshops and mini courses and demonstrations and study groups and seminars and practice sessions and any other settings in which faculty and students could profitably work together to figure out how better to perform whatever services our Community Center set out to provide for its clients. We would place special emphasis on outreach and on counseling with persons who might not ordinarily come for counseling. At the end of two semesters of work and study together, students would receive a master's degree in counseling plus a specialization in cross-cultural counseling.

Return and Re-entry

My colleagues in the Department of Counselor Education to which I returned already knew of my interest in "educational alternatives"—that had been apparent before I left. What they had not previously realized was how committed I was to my rejection of the traditional faculty-student role. So, just as I was returning with my feelings a mixture of anticipation and anxiety, once the initial honeymoon period was over my colleagues began to have their own mixed feelings about my return. Their warm welcome-back to me as a person was mixed with genuine skepticism about, and frequently outright disapproval of, the very ideas that were most important to me.

My professional reputation had been built in part on the original and creative ideas in the numerous proposals for grants and contracts that I had written and the successes of the programs that resulted when they were funded; often my colleagues had been the source of those ideas and always they were the ones who implemented them so successfully in the classroom. During my years as department chair my primary purpose in writing proposals had been to obtain funding to provide the additional time and freedom and resources my colleagues needed in order to try out their own best ideas in their classrooms. Now we found ourselves in a reversal of roles. Now I was asking them to provide an opportunity for me to try out my ideas. My desire to focus on cross-cultural counseling and to work with people of color, they endorsed wholeheartedly; the unorthodox way I insisted that I wanted to go about it presented them with a major dilemma.

I shall always be grateful to my colleagues for the support I received from them throughout that first year. Their respect for our history together outweighed their discomfort over the ideas I now professed. Despite their obvious misgivings, they made it possible for me to go ahead with my dream. It came down to this. If I wanted to do this thing so badly, they were willing to let me give it a try—although none of them personally wanted to work in it with me. I would try it. We would see if it worked.

Throughout 1972-73 they put their misgivings aside and together we initiated an aggressive campaign designed to recruit the diverse group of students I desired. They helped me to find two part-time faculty members, one an African-American and one a Chicano, who were sympathetic to my ideas, to work with me. With their support, the program made its way through official channels and emerged still remarkably consistent with my original dream. By the fall of 1973-74, all would be ready for me to give it a try.

———————

During that first year, events had forced me to make one major change in my dream. The idea that we would operate our own off-campus community counseling center had to be discarded. Once our recruitment and selection process began, we quickly discovered that the very students that we wanted most to recruit were often the ones most likely to need earnings from part-time employment in order to stay in school and hence would not have time to staff our center. Most of them would be able to find part-time employment in inner city agencies or schools so, regretfully, I planned to accept that experience as a substitute.

Incidentally, funding for the rental of facilities for our proposed off-campus center had never been promised either by the university or any other source, but a group of Chicano and African American students and I had developed a plan. We had spent several afternoons driving around southeast and downtown San Diego looking at rentals. We were looking for a large house with large living quarters and lots of rooms, including several bedrooms, located within the inner city that could serve both for communal living and to house our center. The plan had been for me to rent the place (I was now permanently separated from my second wife) and then sublet rooms to students (preferably, but not necessarily exclusively, to students in our program) who were looking for a place for communal living. (The years 1972-73 and 1973-74 were still very much a part of what we loosely call "the sixties" and there were a number of student and non-student communes scattered around the San Diego State campus area in those days.)

When we gave up the idea of the center, we also gave up the idea of starting our own commune. Instead, in the fall of 1973 I rented a smaller house located on a back street in City Heights in a racially mixed neighborhood on the edge of San Diego's major barrio and ghetto areas. The house had a large combined living/dining room area and four bedrooms, and for the next two years it became the off-campus home for the new program. The living/dining area, furnished with borrowed bean bags and folding chairs became our classroom. The one bedroom which was off by itself was mine; the other three became small multi-purpose group rooms, available whenever and however they might be needed. (Those were certainly more innocent times. No one raised questions about legal liability then—university legal departments would clearly be seriously remiss if they failed to do so in today's more litigious climate!)

When CBB first started in the fall of 1973, it looked remarkably consistent with the dream as I described it earlier. It was to be a full-time, year-long graduate program in counseling and it placed heavy emphasis on multicultural issues and cross-cultural counseling. The faculty was racially diverse—an African American, a Chicano, and an Anglo (me)—a pattern that continues to be characteristic of CBB to this day. All three faculty members made a point of being present at all CBB sessions, regardless of the topic under consideration or who might be assuming primary responsibility at any given time. The selection process was based on criteria that were designed to recruit as diverse a group of students as possible by giving top priority to the unique experiences that each student could bring to the total group.

Instead of formal courses and conventional assignments, only two experiences were arbitrarily required of all students. They were the weekly counseling practicum session with live clients under direct observation in the on-campus clinical training facilities, and part-time employment or internship hours in appropriate inner city agencies or schools. This second requirement was added at the time that the idea of operating our own community counseling center was abandoned. Everything else was negotiable, to be determined by community action. Completion of the two semesters of CBB plus two additional courses in summer session would satisfy requirements for the master's degree.

Although CBB had looked at first very much like my original dream, it soon was clear that the program had taken on a life of its own. Major changes were taking place. As reported in the main text, we were able to recruit considerably more persons of color than I had anticipated and this created an entirely different set of dynamics in the group. The loss of a center of our own shifted our curricular focus away from the problems of clients (external) and onto interactions within our own group (internal). Most of my dream had been retained, but the CBB that eventually emerged was all that and so very much more.

II. Proof of the Pudding

Almost from the outset, it seemed clear to those of us directly involved that CBB was becoming all that we had been hoping. . .and more; it would, however, be several years before there would be evidence that would be convincing to critical outsiders. And there *were* critical outsiders. Even though CBB students spent most of their time off campus, they were still highly visible among a student body that in the early 1970s was still almost entirely white. Outsiders did notice. And though little was said to us directly, behind our backs there were those who were thinking, and sometimes saying, that the whole CBB idea was crazy—to admit a group like that (translation: people of color) with those lousy test scores and low GPA's into graduate school in the first place, and then not to have final exams or regular assignments required of them. CBB was causing considerable head-shaking.

CBB survived their negative scrutiny. For the first year or two, supportive evidence was sparse and far from convincing, but as soon as graduates of those first years became established on the job or enrolled in further graduate study, positive reports came pouring in and CBB avoided a premature demise. Three decades later, the program still is going strong; the thirtieth CBB class graduated in June of 2003. Examples of this supportive evidence will be reported later, but first a look at two other relevant early events—the failure of our "A-B-C" project and the success of our women's revolt.

The A-B-C Project

In CBB's first year, practicum groups were organized as "A-B-C" groups ("A" for Anglo, "B" for Black, and "C" for Chicano) so that the "B" and "C" groups could examine conventional counseling approaches and modify (or discard) them as necessary in order to make them more responsive to the needs of persons of color. I had high hopes for the project. I had even (rashly) suggested to my colleagues the likelihood that these groups would produce learning modules, some of which might be incorporated into instruction in the regular counselor education classes.

The trouble was, neither group found anything to report. At some point in the second year the students in effect said to the faculty, "Look, whose program is this? We are not finding anything and we don't like the idea of A-B-C groups, anyway. We think practicum groups should be as diverse as possible so we can all be getting feedback from persons from differing ethnic groups." That was the end of the A-B-C project. Clearly, if we in CBB were to provide the rest of the faculty with reason to continue to support the CBB program, it would not be in the form of neat and readily useable learning modules.

When our A-B-C project failed, I recalled the statement that I mentioned in chapter four by Margaret Mead, that true comparative study of cultures had ended in the 1950s when the transistor radio was born. It had ended because, in her words (at least as I remember them), "on every isolated beach on every remote south sea island, every little native kid now walks along holding a transistor radio to his ear." Acculturation had invaded every remote nook and cranny. No "pure" primitive cultures remained for the anthropologist to study anymore. That had seemed interesting, but not particularly relevant to me at the time. But now, the more I thought about the failure of our A-B-C group project, the more I came to realize that Margaret Mead's complaint was now my own. Small wonder our A-B-C groups found nothing to report. All of our samples were far too contaminated by the idiosyncratic levels of acculturation of the individuals in them.

The failure of the A-B-C group project was an important lesson. It made me realize that I would probably never meet a person of color who wasn't a *mestizo*, a complex and idiosyncratic mixture of cultures. My initial naive and simplistic assumptions about cultural differences were abruptly blasted away. I give this event much of the credit for the more sophisticated understandings that made the final chapters of this book possible. (I mention the failure of our A-B-C group project, not only because of what it contributed to my awareness but also because it is such a good example of CBB in action.)

There was another impactful happening a few semesters later that also is a good example of CBB in action—the women's revolt.

The Women's Revolt

In its second and third years, CBB had an all male faculty. In the third year, there were seventeen women students and only seven men. The seventeen women were an unusually able and outspoken group and at times the outnumbered men appeared overwhelmed by them. In those days my fellow male faculty members and I still had a great deal to learn. In our naiveté none of us sensed the storm that was brewing. We should have. Late in the first semester, the department allocated CBB an additional part-time position to help supervise practicum and field work during the second semester. I said above that we were naive. I should have said naive and insensitive. We offered the position to a male.

We three males brought to the students what we thoughtlessly thought would be welcomed as good news. Wrong. The women revolted. They spoke as one voice. The message they sent was clear. We had hired him. We could simply un-hire him. We said sorry but it was too late for that. They said it was never too late. We tried to stick to our guns. The women went to the university counseling center and invited two specialists on conflict resolution to come and show us how to deal with our deadlock. CBB, faculty and students alike, then spent two days in a workshop on conflict resolution. I am no longer clear about the sequence of events, but at the end of the two days we "un-hired" him. A committee selected by the women then recruited and interviewed additional candidates and recommended that we offer the position to an African-American woman. Which we did.

This women's revolt was not an impulsive or irresponsible act. The women were demonstrating the depth of their involvement and simply assuming responsibility for their own learnings— at a depth that can be reached when students take responsibility for ownership of their own program. If there is any reader not previously clear about what I have meant by students assuming a share of the "ownership" of the turf upon which their learning takes place, these two events ought to make it clear. And if anyone has questioned what I meant about faculty learning from students, let me assure you that we three faculty males learned a great deal from the women's revolt—and that it left us chastened for some time thereafter. Particularly me. It was the first time I had clearly faced the thought that my sexism might be even more deeply ingrained in me than the racism that I abhorred. The women's revolt dramatized for me the persistence of my own insensitivity to gender issues in much the same way that the A-B-C group fiasco had highlighted for me my naiveté about culture and acculturation. To those of us in CBB, both events were clearly positive ones. Still, I can understand how the reports of the revolt that came to outsiders may, like the failure of the A-B-C groups, for some of my colleagues have been a cause for lingering uneasiness.

Still Another Surprise

I had originally thought of CBB as leading to a terminal degree. I had assumed that the program would primarily appeal to persons who had become disenchanted with traditional schools and schooling and that most CBB students would be preparing to move into careers in street agencies and other community services. I had thought that further schooling or even employment in school settings would be among the last things in their minds. Once again CBB proved my original assumptions to be wrong. Although a substantial number of the persons we enrolled were in fact persons who had become disenchanted with schools and schooling, they did not begin to make up a majority. And, what I found even more surprising, many of the very folks who had themselves been most disenchanted, now wanted to work in public schools so that other kids like themselves would not be turned off the way they had been. What's more, after CBB they were willing to return to traditional classrooms and do the further gradu- ate study that was necessary in order to do so.

Over the years, many CBB graduates did find careers in com- munity agencies but an even greater number became counselors in public schools or entered student personnel work at universi- ties, four-year colleges, and community colleges. A substantial number returned after CBB to complete the two-year master's degree required for the Marriage, Family and Child Counseling license in California and other states and became self-employed in private practice as licensed counselors. Others returned to com- plete the three-year master's program leading to the California School Psychologist credential. Several successfully completed doctoral programs at well known universities, including Harvard, Princeton, UCLA, and Johns Hopkins. A number of those who earned their doctorates now hold tenure track university faculty positions, including three who are currently employed at San Di- ego State. But we and our critics would know little or none of this until several years had passed.[23]

The Proof of the Pudding

The proof of the pudding obviously was going to depend on how well CBB graduates who went directly into the world of

---

[23] In a survey conducted in 1993 of graduates of the first twenty CBB classes, out of 556 total graduates 332 respondents listed their current work settings as follows: agencies (public/private) 106; schools (elemen- tary and secondary) 88; community colleges 61; universities/four-year colleges 33; private practice/self-employed 38; other 22. (The total num- ber here slightly exceeds 332 because 16 respondents listed themselves as employed in more than one setting.) The same survey found that while most CBB graduates had remained in California, they were also employed in 24 other states plus the District of Columbia and as civil- ians at three overseas military bases.

work performed on the job and how well those who continued on for further graduate study performed in the classroom. Evidence that CBB graduates were successful in both settings was not long in coming. Graduates of Year One and Year Two readily found jobs in a wide variety of settings and performed so well on the job that by the time the third CBB class graduated, employers were already becoming eager to hire more CBB graduates.

One employer in particular deserves special mention. The late Fran Patterson, then Director of the District Counselor program for San Diego Unified School District, hired two CBB graduates from Year Two and two more from Year Three. These four graduates performed so well on the job that the following year her department hired no less than eight—one-third of the twenty-four CBB graduates of Year Four. No one could ask for evidence of employer satisfaction more convincing than this. (In 1998, more than twenty years later, one of those first twelve CBB graduates hired by Fran Patterson was deceased but the other eleven were still employed fulltime in the San Diego Unified School District!)

The following vignettes will suggest some of the reasons why employers so soon came to hold CBB graduates in such high regard.

Molly

When a counselor in an inner city agency primarily serving young African-American adults was transferred to another office in mid-year, Molly was one of two half-time hourly counselors hired as his replacement. Molly was Anglo, blond, attractive, one of the youngest CBB graduates of the year before, looking even younger than her actual years. When she first told me that she had been offered the job, I couldn't help wondering whether anyone as young and white as she was would survive in that particular job setting. Some time later I was attending a meeting at which Molly's supervisor was present. When I asked how Molly was doing, her supervisor gave her rave reviews. Molly fitted in easily, she found things to do, she took initiative, she needed minimal supervision. By contrast, the supervisor told me, the other new counselor, both older and male (and not from CBB!), still seemed insecure, still often had to be told exactly what to do.

When I told Molly about the compliment, she replied, "You know why that is, don't you? It's all due to CBB. Last year if we hadn't learned to take over and figure out what to do for ourselves, we would never have learned anything!"

Miguel

Upon graduation from CBB, Miguel was offered a counseling position in a large community college in central California. He was very much interested in the job because the college enrolled a large Chicano population, but he hesitated about accepting because during his visit to the campus he had observed that the counselors already employed there were not doing much if any personal counseling. Miguel talked with me at length about his dilemma. He said that he did not want to spend his professional life mostly making changes in students' programs. Yet he wanted to be working where his people were. In the end he decided to give it a try.

Eighteen months or so later I got a letter from Miguel. In it he happily reported that at least 60 percent of his time was being spent in personal counseling. What's more, once he had broken the ice, three or four of the other counselors had begun to do substantially more personal counseling as well. The reason he wrote me, he said, was because he had just returned from a session with his boss who had gone out of her way to compliment him both on the job he was doing and on having made so great an impact on the entire counseling program in such a short time.

Kay

Three and a half years after her graduation from CBB, Kay—a young, energetic, enthusiastic African-American woman—was highly regarded by her supervisors as a successful secondary school counselor. Here, verbatim, are the comments Kay wrote in response to a follow-up request that I had sent out asking graduates how they now felt about CBB and what they thought were the most important things about the program. Kay wrote: "Willing commitment to learn from experiences shared with others. *Know* that I loved it and would not have had a better learning experience from any other program known to me. Good luck to you and the future grads of the Community-Based Block. *I can handle anything!*" (Emphasis hers.)

There was general agreement among CBB graduates who went on into advanced graduate study, including doctoral programs, that they had found the going somewhat difficult at first because they were not as familiar as many of their new fellow students with much of the vocabulary and many of the concepts that were being discussed. But, they reported, the gap soon closed. Many insisted, a bit immodestly perhaps, that not only did it not take long, but also that once they did pick up the terminology and grasp the concepts, they understood them better than their fellow students did because their CBB experiences had instilled in them the habit of questioning when ideas made sense and when they did not. I know my sample is probably far from complete, but in the more than twenty-five years that have gone by I have yet to talk with or hear about a single CBB graduate who went on into doctoral study who expressed any regret at having gone through CBB first.

Meanwhile, more immediate reports were coming in from a source closer to home—the performance of CBB students who continued on in classes at SDSU—and these reports, like the reports about graduates on the job, were consistently positive. Within three or four years the misgivings about CBB that initially had been prevalent among our own faculty not only seemed to have disappeared but actually seemed to have been forgotten. Faculty members repeatedly told me how much they were enjoying having CBB graduates in their classes. The school counselor credential program (which was lengthened to a two-year program at about this time) and the school psychologist credential program began actively to recruit CBB students. Indeed, the SDSU school psychology program was ultimately to achieve national recognition as an outstanding program for training students from a variety of ethnic backgrounds to work with multi-ethnic school populations—a level of prominence the program might never have been able to achieve without the boost it got from having CBB to provide it with a steady supply of able students of color.

Favorable faculty comments about CBB graduates were not limited to faculty from my own department. Two that I remember vividly—and for very different reasons—merit mention here. Both were from faculty members who taught the courses in research and statistics that were required of degree candidates from all the departments in the SDSU College of Education.

A Different Kind of Questions

In the first of the two instances, the professor came up to me one day and said, "Dave, recently I have been having two or three of your CBB students in my classes each semester and it has been a real pleasure having them." Thinking of their year in the more informal atmosphere of CBB, I replied, "I imagine that they speak out in class a lot more than the regular students do." "No," he said, "Not more, just different. They ask a different kind of questions. The regular students speak out just as much, but the questions they ask are more likely to be something like, 'Would you go over that stuff you presented last week for us again?' or 'Is the material in this week's chapter going to be on the final exam?' Your CBB folks on the other hand are more likely to ask me, 'How many African-Americans were there in that sample?' or 'How do you know that?' They make me think."

Smart Students of Color

The other professor told me, "Dave, I've got five of your CBB students in my classes this semester and they are all doing well. I hope this doesn't sound racist (it did!), but I am not used to having students of color do well in my classes. Usually the blacks drop out after a few weeks. Chicanos usually manage to stick it out somehow and just squeak by in the end with low B's. So it is really a special delight for me to have so many smart students of color all at once."

I don't remember what I may have said to him at the time but it probably was not what I was thinking. I do remember that I went to the registrar's office and asked to see his class lists so I could find out who these "bright" students were. It turned out that he actually had six CBB folks in his two sections, and five of the six had initially been denied admission to graduate study. To get them admitted the department had to submit formal petitions for a waiver of either a low grade point average or a low graduate record exam score or, in some cases, both. The professor was correct in one respect. They were smart students. But the graduate admissions office certainly would never have suspected it.

The Community-Based Block had started out in 1973-74 on a let's-try-it-and-see basis. Within four or five years it had firmly established itself in the college and in the community. In fact, in many respects it quickly became one of the things of which the college was very proud. Credit for all this is strictly due to the reputation CBB graduates were making for themselves in their jobs in the community and in the classes they took on the university campus. Few any longer were raising questions about our unorthodox pedagogy even though supportive data were still largely anecdotal in nature.

During 1977-78, however, thanks to a grant obtained from the CSU Fund for "Innovation in the Instructional Process," CBB was reviewed by two external evaluators, both widely respected counselor educators and both chairs at urban universities with large counselor education programs. Each evaluator independently visited CBB for two days, interviewing students, graduates, field supervisors, employers of graduates, and university faculty. Now, for the first time, objective, impartial evaluative data about CBB became available. Both evaluators submitted highly favorable reports. One of them concluded his report as follows:

(CBB). . .in my judgment, represents a challenge to existing programs not only in the field of counselor education, but perhaps in other disciplines as well. It demonstrates that the selection criteria we use. . .in a traditionally-oriented degree program. . .may not necessarily be the best, or at least not the only, criteria for selecting people who can function effectively in a practical situation.

"It raises questions in my mind about whether traditional programs are leaving untapped, reservoirs of motivation, autonomy and responsibility in their students. Students who function well in highly structured, highly monitored programs don't necessarily learn the kinds of skills that are functional on jobs. These (CBB) students do seem to learn them, in this kind of program. Perhaps treating students as mature, responsible, self-determining individuals does really leave an impact upon their motivation and their performance. Perhaps the gate-keeping function of graduate schools has become more important than the teaching function.

The writer of these paragraphs, Professor Earl Carnes, long-time Chair of the Department of Counselor Education at the University of Southern California, summed up his impressions of CBB in a conversation with a mutual friend in my presence. "Jean," he said to her, "that program has no right to get the results it is getting!"

Clearly, despite the misgivings of many, as early as 1978, CBB had gotten itself well under way.

One important aside before I continue. The CBB I am writing about at this point is CBB as I lived it during the first nineteen years of its existence, the nineteen years that I was directly involved in it. My nineteen years already is less than two-thirds of the now more than thirty years of CBB. (2002-03 was CBB's 30th year.) There have been changes in CBB since my departure just as there were changes from time to time while I was there. Change is built in. Each new year in a very literal sense CBB opens "under new management," faculty and student. Some of the details that I mention may have changed or at least been slightly modified since my time. One thing I do know. I do know that so far the basic *sabor* (flavor, essence) of CBB has not changed. I have kept in touch closely enough to be able to vouch for that.

III. The "Sabor" of CBB

In the remainder of this postscript, I will attempt to offer a few more glimpses of what goes on inside CBB in hopes of providing at least some feel for its true *sabor*.(How about that— glimpses, feel, *sabor*—all in one mixed metaphor!) To do so, it will be helpful first to describe the special roles that power and structure play in CBB, so first a few words about each of them.

The Role of Power

Arguably, the school classroom—be it public or private, elementary, secondary or higher education—is one of the least democratic institutions in America. The classroom teacher traditionally wields enormous arbitrary power over the subjects in her/his own small fiefdom. Control of the gate-keeping function is placed in the teacher's hands and there is a saying that, "trying to change a teacher's grade is like trying to move a graveyard." With the possible exception of the military, a classroom teacher's power is about as near to absolute as is likely to be found in American democracy. Since there is no place for this kind of power in the CBB community-partnership, shared ownership model, CBB faculty voluntarily give it up.

Notice that I say "this kind of power." There are two very different kinds of power—"position" power and "personal" power. Position power (or authority) is power that is inherent in the position and is not transportable. When a teacher leaves a position, this power does not go with her/him; when a new person takes over the position, this power automatically becomes hers/his. Personal power (or potency) is a totally different matter. (More about personal power later.)

The power that CBB faculty give up in order to enter into a partnership relationship is position power. This is one area that has been modified a bit. For the first fifteen years or so, CBB faculty did give up this power entirely. In more recent years, as our society has become increasingly litigious and students participating in field work and practicum have themselves been required to obtain personal liability insurance, CBB faculty have been forced to retain some limited traditional arbitrary powers in those situations in which they are deemed to be legally responsible and can personally be held to be liable. CBB students appear to have understood and accepted this change; clearly it has not destroyed their sense of shared ownership as I originally had feared that it would.

The Role of Structure

A second issue is the role of "structure" in CBB—or, as some would maintain, the lack thereof. Because CBB faculty members give up the position power which traditionally permits them to call all the shots, CBB has sometimes been thought of as unstructured. This is totally in error. Although its structure may not be as immediately apparent because it is so different, CBB is not without structure. It has a structure distinctly its own—a structure that differs from the familiar classroom significantly in at least three aspects. First, the structure of CBB is democratic in the sense that all members, students and faculty alike, have an equal voice in decision-making—but at the same time somewhat libertarian in that there are no formal mechanisms to enforce decisions made by majority vote. Second, CBB admissions criteria ensure a pluralistic community in which no one group (except in the case of gender) will be a majority and in which there will be wide diversity in values and opinions. Thus confrontation and conflict are built in. Third, instead of resolution of conflict by faculty authority or by majority vote, CBB structure provides the community meeting as the vehicle for decision-making. Students are motivated to reach consensus mainly because of their shared goal of becoming effective counselors.

When the Shoe Is on the Other Foot

The white students in CBB each year quickly discover how frequently they are stereotyped as whites and not reacted to as individuals by people of color. . .and they don't like it. The typical reaction is to feel angry, hurt, resentful, not appreciated, not respected. They grumble in protest that "all whites are not alike," that "even though we are all white, some of us have very little in common with each other," that "we are not all oppressors," and that "it's not fair to lump good whites with other whites who may have committed overt atrocities." The hurt at being treated so unfairly— "They shouldn't feel that way about us!"—is so nearly universal that it usually takes some time before the realization sets in that they are only being done unto what Anglos have been doing to people of color for generations. The shoe was now on the other foot. It was now the Anglo turn to experience how it feels.

For some white students, the initial reaction is a tendency simply to bail out—the "if they don't appreciate me, the hell with them" response. Others show almost exactly the opposite reaction, a tendency toward the syndrome known as "white guilt" which, when carried to its extreme can amount to overwhelming feelings of guilt, shame and even self-hatred. In the intimate give-and-take of the CBB community, neither of these views survives very long. At this point it becomes a learning experience that marks a long step forward toward progress in mutual understanding. (Within the larger society, "the-hell-with-them" and "white guilt" are all too familiar white responses to their typically limited level of interaction with other groups—regrettably, usually without opportunity for the healthy follow-up experiences that occur in CBB.)

Ethnic Presentations

In CBB, moments of intensity and intimacy are by no means limited to dealing with matters of personal crisis. Typically each year the various ethnic/cultural groups make presentations before the rest of the community, sharing significant, sometimes little known aspects of their group's cultural heritage and mores.

Always these presentations have been informative and frequently they have been very personal and moving. Sometimes they were humorous as well, like on the day when the rest of us returned from lunch only to find the four Filipino students who were to make a presentation that afternoon perched up in the branches of two small trees near the doorway to our meeting place. They started their presentation still in the trees, chattering to each other and refusing to come down, explaining that since other folks consider Filipinos to be more monkey-like than human anyway, they felt obliged to live up to our expectations.

On several occasions, African-Americans included in their presentation reading or reciting powerful selections from Black poets and, in some cases, reciting deeply personal poetry they had written themselves. Latinas have told about their still raw pain from the loss of brothers or boyfriends in gang shootings. Several times Native American Indians began their presentation on religious aspects of their world by first going slowly around our room "purifying" the space with the incense of burning native sage. The combination of valuable informative content and intensely intimate moments in these presentations exemplifies the true *sabor* of CBB.

This same burning sage ritual was not exactly a success when a group of us, led by a Native American Indian, visited my CBB colleague Raymond Howard in the hospital and began burning sage to purify his room for him. Bells rang and nurses descended upon us from all directions and we and our ceremonial sage were unceremoniously ushered out.

The Impact of CBB

Graduates often remark that they did not realize how much they had learned during CBB until after they had left it. This is at least in part because the impact that CBB has on its members is based on the total CBB experience and derives every bit as much from *how* students learn as it does from *what* students learn. The story of Cindy is a case in point. She was a bright and outspoken Anglo in her late twenties who found CBB to be a disappointment and openly said so throughout much of the fall semester. She complained about the "endless community meetings that never got anything done" and asked, "When are we going to learn something? All these ethnic presentations and workshops and guest speakers are great and all that, but when are we going to get to some real learning?"

After spending her Christmas holidays at her parents' home in a city some distance away, Cindy returned at the start of the second semester singing a very different tune. "I'm the one who thought I wasn't learning anything in CBB," she told us. "When I got back home and sat down to watch TV with my parents, I couldn't believe the racist comments they were making. I couldn't believe how sexist the TV programs were. Even when I was out with my friends, I couldn't believe how uninformed and bigoted they were. It wasn't easy for me to keep my mouth shut. I could hardly wait to get back to San Diego, and I don't think they were real sorry when I left, either. And to think that before CBB, I used to just sit there and not even notice!"

Cindy's story, while a bit more dramatic (and painful) than most, otherwise is not atypical. It clearly shows that in CBB the impact comes from learnings that result from the total CBB experience, not solely from the presentation of individual bits of specific blocks of subject matter. CBBers find they are looking at the world through new eyes.

The examples reported earlier of Molly, Miguel and Kay also illustrate the impact that results from the total CBB experience. Molly took initiative, found things to do, needed minimum supervision. Miguel could report after eighteen months on a new job that he had brought about important changes in the entire counseling program in the community college at which he worked. Kay could confidently exclaim that, "I can handle anything!" Of course, none of them would have been as successful as they were without solid skills and knowledge and information, but it was not those attributes, but rather other intangibles that marked them out from the others with whom they worked. Cindy is an example of the self-discovery that CBB promotes; Molly, Miguel, and Kay exemplify the personal power that such self-discovery releases.

About Personal Power

What made Molly, Miguel and Kay (and dozens and dozens of other CBB graduates like them—including Cindy, by the way—

so special was their own personal power or personal potency (I use the terms interchangeably), the power or potency which resides within one's own person. It was not position power. Position power can only be used to serve the purposes of the system that supports it. Personal power is the only form of power that can be used to bring about change within a system. For this reason, personal power is by its very nature threatening to position power and sometimes may be vigorously suppressed by it! While personal potency springs from a variety of sources (including skills, knowledge, and information), the key to its release lies in the sort of self-discovery so characteristic of CBB.

Jessica

CBB students benefit from the ever-enlarging CBB network when they look for employment. Graduates are quick to let CBB faculty know whenever openings occur and increasingly they are being promoted into positions where they have major input into the hiring process. Here is just one example. At the time that Jessica, an Anglo, was hired as a full time, tenure-track counselor at a large community college, not one of her fellow counselors was a person of color even though the college served a diverse student body. When she asked why this was so, she was told that they would indeed have liked to have hired some persons of color and that they knew that they needed to, but they simply had never been able to find any who were qualified.

Jessica had heard that story from her fellow CBBers before so she asked to be put on the selection committee. The next time there was an opening, Jessica sent word to other CBBers. Some time later she called to tell me not only that the position had been offered to a person of color but that of the five finalists, four had been people of color (three of them from CBB) and that the selection committee (of which she was a member) had agreed that they would gladly have hired all four of them if they had been able to do so.

Jessica was not alone. Today there are CBB graduates among the counselors at every community college in San Diego County and at numerous others throughout the state, and one is now president of a community college in central California. Many school districts, including San Diego Unified School District and

Sweetwater Union High School District have numerous CBB graduates on their staffs. A number of CBBers now hold supervisory positions in various community agencies. At the time of the celebration of the graduation of the twentieth CBB class in 1993, current zip code information was available for 447 of the 556 persons who had completed CBB; of these, 179 were in the city of San Diego, 128 in other parts of San Diego County, and an additional 91 elsewhere in California.

Each year the graduates of one more class join its ranks and keep the CBB network alive and thriving—and continuing to transcend color and ethnic lines.

Appendix B

Text of presentation by Dave Malcolm at the celebration
of the CBB Thirtieth Anniversary, May 10, 2003

That Dream of Mine That Started the Whole CBB Thing

People often call me "the father of CBB" and I feel very proud when they do because I know that what they really mean is that the origin of CBB was my personal dream. At the same time, I always want to point out that my CBB dream was not something spun out of thin air that I just sat back in an easy chair and dreamed up. It was instead the product of my own interactions with the world around me over a period of many years. Sometimes in retrospect I almost feel as if I have been only a leaf being carried along by a great river.

Believe it or not, for me the story of CBB goes back to 1958 when Sputnik, the Russian satellite, went up and showed the world how far the Russians were ahead of the USA in the race into space. You see Sputnik caused the U. S. Congress in its wisdom to pass something that came to be known as the National Defense Education tion Act (NDEA), an act originally designed mainly to improve science and math teaching in American schools so we could catch up with the Russians.

But it seems that there was a very powerful senior senator from Oregon named Wayne Morse who was the chair of a very important senate committee, and it further seems that when Wayne Morse was a kid in high school there was a counselor who gave him some advice that had changed his entire life, and so this Sena-

tor Wayne Morse absolutely refused to let that NDEA bill out of his committee unless they put a nice fat pot of money into it to provide for the training of more counselors. Which Congress did.

And it turns out that San Diego State was one of the colleges fortunate enough to get quite a lot of that money, and since the federal government was paying the entire cost, this expensive new program had to be, and I quote "required of, and limited to" students specially recruited for that program. In other words it had to be an intact block program. So all during the sixties San Diego State conducted these federally funded counselor education programs and that's the history of how and where I first learned the potential of the block type of program which I simply copied for CBB, something of course I never could have done if it hadn't been for Sputnik, NDEA, and Wayne Morse.

But other things important to the history of CBB were also happening to me during those same years. I am referring especially to the counter culture/youth movements of the sixties. I had been profoundly influenced by the idealism of the Youth of the '60s, among them my oldest children who in various ways were deeply involved in the counterculture movement and by my graduate students, especially those in our NDEA Institutes who, it so frequently turned out, knew and could do things that I and other faculty members knew little or nothing about.

My children and my students were into a world strange and new to me. They were into Carlos Castaneda, the I Ching, Zen, Sufi, American Indian lore, Tai Chi, psychedelics, Esalen, Eastern religions, Marcuse, Anais Nin, Ram Dass, Lorca, Theodore Roszak, Ken Kesey, Paulo Freire, Alvin Toffler, Ivan Illich, the Beatles and the Beats...the list goes on and on—all realms unnervingly unfamiliar to me and to my peers.

By the fall of 1970 when I went on a sabbatical, I was increasingly uncomfortable with the idea of returning to the conventional faculty role which defined my relationship with students strictly as one in which they should come to learn from me when I now strongly suspected that often I had as much or more to learn from some of them. Clearly the events of the sixties are reflected in much of my CBB dream—in particular in the faculty/student relationship.

In the fall of 1970, prior to my sabbatical leave, I was an Anglo male university professor who had lived for my almost 54 years in what to all intents and purposes always had been and still was a virtually lily-white world. My friends and my associates and my students and my campus and my neighborhood all were still almost entirely white. In the next two years all this was abruptly to change.

In Washington, D. C., the federal funds that originally had been designated for the broad purpose of educating more counselors now were about to be targeted more specifically to strengthen programs at institutions that previously had been unable to compete successfully for funds and to bring "more members of underrepresented groups" (code words for "people of color") into graduate level training programs.

In some instances this meant making grants to institutions with little or no prior experience in managing federally funded contracts, so it was decided that the services of an external consultant should be provided. I was on sabbatical leave so I was available. I was experienced and I was well regarded in the Office of Education. I had been employed by the USOE as a consultant before. Result: early in my sabbatical year, I became an external consultant. Apparently, no one, including me, had given any thought to the fact that I had no expertise and little prior experience in working with people of color. Clearly I was in for a cultural plunge!

Thus, unprepared as I was, early in 1971 I took on the job as external consultant and extended my leave for an additional year. Suddenly my world was filled with people of color. I worked with Chicanos in the southwest, Native American Indians in the northwest, and African-Americans in a number of large eastern and north central urban centers. Most of my time, however, I spent in the five southeastern states—Alabama, Florida, Georgia, Mississippi and Tennessee. My year and a half in the job was packed with new experiences. Despite my numerous blunders and my naïveté about people of color (I had never even heard of Marvin Gaye!), my work as a consultant turned out to be both satisfying and successful.

As I look back on that year and a half, I still find it hard to believe that one as naive and as inexperienced in working with people of color as I was then managed to survive at all, much less to be so generously accepted and so generally successful. I think I was accepted largely because I came to the job realizing that I had at least as much to learn from the people with whom I was to work as they did from me. At the same time I was not at all certain how relevant the things I knew would be to them but I was hoping that I could contribute something worthwhile. All these, you will note, were the very attitudes that I had developed as a result of my experiences with the youth movement during the turbulent years of the sixties.

Clearly I did learn a great deal from those with whom I worked; equally clearly, I did make a contribution which was valued by them since they continued to retain my services out of their own budgets as a part-time consultant for several semesters after my leave had ended. Ours had been a symbiotic relationship. They had known things I wouldn't have known and I had known things they wouldn't have known and together we became a productive partnership.

My leave ended at the end of the summer of 1972 and I returned to San Diego State. I now appreciated how satisfying and productive a symbiotic partnership could be and a dream began to emerge of teaching in a program in which this same symbiotic partnership would exist between faculty and students. The details were far from clear in my mind but at least I knew the role that I wanted to play and I knew that I wanted it to involve people of color.

As I have written in the booklet, The CBB Story, "My original idea, if not an impossible dream was certainly an immodest one. My intentions were clear even though the details were still vague. I sincerely believed that what I had in mind would produce a better program for training counselors than any program I had ever developed before.

"What I wanted to do was create a 'learning community' in which faculty and students would relate with each other the way I had related with the folks with whom I had been working as a consultant during my leave—as equal partners working side by side on some important task. The important task I had in mind was cross-cultural counseling."

So there you have it. There you have the story behind the dream with which I returned from my sabbatical in 1972, the dream upon which CBB as we know it today was built. But there is one thing more that I want to point out. CBB as it exists today in many ways is much different from and very much more than my original dream. Yes, I was the dreamer and I started it, but I didn't build it alone. To a great extent the CBB that exists today was built by the hundreds of students who have gone through it during its first thirty years.

You see, change is built into CBB—each new year in a very literal sense CBB reopens under new ownership. (Maybe CBB ought to hang out a sign each September!) But it has been thirty years now and in three basic respects CBB has not changed. It still is an intact group in a year-long learning community, it still is faculty and students working together as partners sharing ownership, and its task still is developing skills in cross-cultural counseling. All three of which are traceable to that dream of mine that owed so much to our NDEA Institutes, to the youth movement of the sixties, and to my consulting work with people of color. Without any one of these three, CBB wouldn't be CBB!

Index

Educated at Phillips Exeter Academy and Harvard, Boston and Northwestern Universities, Dave Malcolm was a high-school English teacher, coach, journalist and Navy Lieutenant prior to joining the faculty at Wisconsin State College in Milwaukee in 1948. From 1953 to 1992, he taught at San Diego State University, where he chaired the Department of Counselor Education for twelve years and was the Director of the Community-Based Block for nineteen.

Dave has been the recipient of numerous grants, contracts and consultancies with the U. S. Office of Education and other state and federal agencies. In the 1970s, he consulted at 35 universities in 23 states, working to bring more persons of color into higher education. In 1985, he was Project Director, Vienna Peace Project at Rust, Austria, cosponsored by Universidad para la Paz, Escazu, Costa Rica; the Carl Rogers Institute for Peace, La Jolla, California; and the Austrian Society for Foreign Policy and International Relations, Vienna, Austria.

Dave is retired and lives in San Diego, California.